WHAT OTHERS ARE SAYING

"One of my favorite parts of David's book is his interpretation of Simon Sinek's famous question, What is your Why? As a physical therapist and having the life experience of being a staff therapist then business owner, David delivers his story from the unique perspective of someone who has lived the professional experiences we encounter every day. He understands the pressures of being a clinician and treating patients while maintaining the challenges of taking the leap of faith when it comes to starting a business. He understands the fears and frustrations we all experience and can convey his experiences in a way that resonates with me as a therapist.

As a practice owner and treating therapist myself, I can say that this book would have been a foundational text for me and required reading on the journey from burnt-out staff therapist ready to switch careers to being a thriving and happy practice owner enjoying and cherishing the time freedom I now possess. Additionally, knowing that the business I have built not only helps my patients to optimize their quality of life, but also gives clinicians a platform to succeed and to achieve their goals."

- Anthony Maritato, PT, Clinic Owner

"If there is an expert on the topic of a winning mindset, it's David Bayliff! Undoubtedly, he has mastered confidence in his own abilities and in building his successful business. When one interacts with him in person or online, it becomes clear very quickly that this guy lights up a room and sparks major positivity towards everyone around him. So, if you are looking for a book that inspires you and helps you create the right mindset to build or to grow the business of your dreams, this is the book for you. It's full of all sorts of inspiration and examples of how to apply powerful mindset principles. David delivers the information in a fun and easy-flowing way with actionable steps you can take immediately."

- Tracy Sher, PT, National Acclaimed Pelvic Guru

"David is one of the original pioneers of mobile physical therapy. There may have been others before him, but he is one of the first to lay out his process and systems for starting and growing a thriving mobile cash practice. I've had the pleasure of working with David, and it's been a highlight of my young career. He is one of the most knowledgeable, kind, and thoughtful leaders in the physical therapy world. Most people want to hold on to what has made them successful and keep it for themselves, but not David. His generous nature and willingness to help others has sparked dozens, if not hundreds, of people into starting their mobile therapy practices. If you are looking for a way to practice on your terms and set your own value as a provider, this is an absolute must read!"

-Will Boyd, DPT
Co-owner of Healthcare Digital Marketing – leaders in the healthcare profession for coaching providers in developing a strong and effective social media presence in order to grow their own business.

"The book you are holding has the ability to completely change the trajectory of your life by starting with what is between your ears. A must-read to make this the best year yet in your physical therapy career."

- Josh Payne, DPT
Physical Therapist business coach, and author of The Concierge PT Success Formula

"Captain Bayliff is one of my few heroes I look to for wisdom. I don't use the word 'Hero' lightly.

I have had multiple opportunities to learn about Life from this giant giver. I gain true Joy from depth of the Truths that he drops on me. His ability to help me to see the realization of gratitude I have is a Blessing. The Captain is a master at helping people to right their own ship, and to find the treasure of self-confidence as they step into their highest potential."

~Alex Engar
Co-owner of Healthcare Digital Marketing – leaders in healthcare for helping professionals to develop a strong and effective social media presence in order to grow their own business.

THE WINNING MINDSET FOR THE MOBILE ENTREPRENEUR

Mary Beth

While intentional Action steps
are key in finding success, doing
so with the right mindset)
is a must.

Remember, If you aint first,
you're last!

Best wishes,
Dave

THE WINNING MINDSET FOR THE MOBILE ENTREPRENEUR
MOBILE ENTREPRENEUR
SUCCESS STARTS BETWEEN THE EARS

David Bayliff, PT, MPT

DEDICATION

My Purdy Little Lady, Miss Cara.

She patiently sipped on red blend, Garnacha, and Pinot Noir while watching various "Housewives of Somewhere" shows during this whole process.

She lovingly supports me throughout my endeavors that often take time away from us, so that I can create more time for us.

Thank you for believing in me!

 I love you!

This book was written with the infusion of the author's personality.

Table of Contents

FOREWORD

.....For over two decades I've known David. From Tennis to Rehabilitation, he has created a vibe of self-awareness for one to maximize and potentiate their talent to reach their goals and dreams. He does a fantastic job of spelling out and describing how to overcome obstacles of the traditional medical business mindset and becoming an entrepreneur and thinking outside of the box.

I've had a very successful sports medicine practice nearly 22 years and it has centered on a nontraditional business model. Under that scope i have had the opportunity to not only advise, but coach many physicians in the medical field on how to think outside of the box. David has implemented similar steps on how to execute what it takes to stay ahead of the game in this dynamic field.

After completing David's book, you will have a blueprint on how to think outside the box and build your legacy as a mobile entrepreneur in the field of physical therapy and rehabilitation. That blueprint is centered on finding that passion in your career and developing your avatar of yourself and creating a self-awareness that you can leverage and pass on to others. You will have all the tools that you need to build your legacy and tribe in the field of physical therapy and rehabilitation.

David G Carfagno DO, CAQSM
Scottsdale Sports Medicine

ACKNOWLEDGEMENTS

The Entrepreneurial Journey is very rarely traveled alone. Mine surely has not been solo. Everyone needs their Inspiration, their Muse, their Coach, and their "Why" in order to sniff the full potential on the reason for which they walk the earth.

I am so grateful for my family who has given me the space to complete this project.

To my wife, Cara, for her understanding. Of course, she MAY have been equally as grateful to have the time to catch up on her tv shows, and go on Hallmark movie marathons. Now I owe her a marathon of time.

To my offspring, Reece and Sydney. You two are my Reason, my Inspiration. But, hey, guys, while you are holding this book in your hands, remember: I told you that I'm a pretty big deal.

To my mentor, Greg Todd. You sold me with your first voice message reply in January 2018. You have changed my life 1000%. I can't even begin to express my gratitude. Thank you for your relentless efforts to help others to achieve their potential. The world is a better place because of you. I love you, brother. And to Mrs. Todd, thank you for sharing your husband with us. YOU are his rock.

To Alex Engar and Will Boyd, aka "A&W". You fellas have helped me to grow more than you can imagine. Your coaching has helped me to overcome my own Limiting Beliefs. I owe the fact that I even started coaching as a business to you two. You showed me what was possible. Thank you.

To my fellow Demon Deacon, F. Scott Feil.
You have been my offensive line in growing The Mobile PT LEAGUE. I have had many doors open because of your work in the trenches.

Thank you to my business partner and friend, Josh Payne.
Your fire pushes me to COMPETE EVERYDAY. They say that if you can't run with the Big Dogs, don't get off the porch. Thank you for inspiring me to get off the porch.

To Jeremy Sutton, my "Kick in the Arse" for getting this book written. Thank you for everything you did to help me to complete the book. When I had my doubts, you fired me up! When I didn't write, you called me out. Your excitement for this project pushed me to get it done! Thank you!! Love you, bro!

To the SSPTNATION. Simply, the best freakin tribe anyone could possibly have. You all inspire me to be better each and every day. Thank you!

And finally, to my little dog, Yuki. You encouraged me and comforted me by lying in the office entryway while I racked my brains.

SUCCESS STARTS BETWEEN THE EARS

Building a successful business requires taking well-constructed and proven action steps. Without action, dreams are simply ideas. Action moves things forward. Action turns dreams into reality. The mere act of taking a step involves making the conscious decision to do something differently. That decision involves a thought. Therefore, success starts between the ears.

INTRODUCTION

Let me start by saying that businesses are more alike than they are different. That's right. Businesses are more alike than they are different. Whether you are growing your own mobile healthcare related practice, starting a brick-and-mortar clinic, operate a granite countertop business, selling kitchen cabinets, own a gym or cross fit box, manage a restaurant, or you happen to have a large multimillion (even billion) dollar industry, the principles that are needed in order to achieve success are the same. Businesses are more alike than they are different. That is something to keep in mind as you are reading this book.

As you are beginning your own business, the principles outlined in this book will apply to you; regardless of the industry you may be serving. If you are a healthcare provider, as I am, the principles are the same whether you are a brick-and-mortar practice, or a mobile practice. For ALL businesses, the primary goal is not only about attracting clients, but is also about retaining those clients. The ultimate goal is to develop "raging fans" that want to support your business. Depending on your business, Growth does not always mean a constant stream of NEW clients. Growth can very well be optimizing the opportunities with the clients you currently have.

I have been a practicing physical therapist since 1994. I have worked in the hospital setting and for various outpatient orthopedic clinics. I have always loved what I do. In fact, if I wasn't serving people through physical therapy, I honestly do not know what else I would be doing. It truly fulfills me.

Let me stop for one moment and ask a favor of you. Read the previous two sentences again:

If I wasn't serving people through physical therapy, I honestly do not know what else I would be doing. It truly fulfills me.

These two sentences right here are a foreshadowing of what you are going to learn for starting your own business.

Life in an outpatient physical therapy clinic can be rather hectic and time intensive. Most clinics will schedule 3-4 clients per hour for each therapist. Yes, a few clinics are developing a scheduling model of one client every 45 minutes. But, a vast majority of clinics are, as we call them, "mills".

In the clinics where I practiced, I would typically see 24-32 clients in a 10-hour workday. This always translated into a solid 1.5 to 2 hours of paperwork. I eventually found myself spending close to 14 hours a day in the clinic. The long hours had led to divorce. Life as I wanted to enjoy it no longer existed, because my life was lived in the clinic.

I can recall being with a client one afternoon trying to focus on their report of their current physical status. But my attention was constantly being redirected towards the gym floor where there were three other patients struggling to perform exercises. I knew that all three would soon be ready for my hands-on care. A quick glance to the waiting room was a reminder that my next scheduled client was waiting. Meanwhile, the receptionist was standing beside me with the news that my new client was now ready for me. New client? What new client? Oh, yeah, the one that the front desk forgot to inform me that they had squeezed into my day. And, of course, mounds of paperwork awaited me. The grind was finally getting to me after 19 years.

I was 45 years old at the time. My first thought was "This sucks." My second thought was "I do not want to be a 50-year-old staff clinician." The last thing that ran through my mind was that this was not a life. But I had two problems. The first was that I had previously served as a clinic director for another large clinic. The time involved with that had led to my divorce. Starting a clinic would be even more intensive and time consuming, and that was a fire that I was not about to start. Secondly, I still loved what I did. That left me not knowing where to go. Until one day I received a call that would change everything.

I had been treating several clients of a particular concierge MD in town. The physician called me one day to ask if I would be willing to see one of her clients in his home. This was a wealthy individual who preferred to have all services and businesses come to him. She assured me that this gentleman was willing to pay me directly. Since I knew that I had two mornings a week free, I agreed to do so.

I will admit that seeing a high number of clients each day for years had me a little worried that I would be able to "come up" with something to do with one person for a full hour. However, it was much to my delight that the hour seemed to fly quickly. I noticed how relaxing it was to not have 13 other distractions and I could focus on the person before me. There was no yelling to others across the gym floor. I did not have a surprise evaluation thrown on me. The hour was nothing but pure calmness. It was heaven. When I left the gentleman's house, I knew exactly what my next move would be.

Sometimes, identifying your path in order to pursue your dreams involves being open to an opportunity. Everyone can feel stuck and uncertain as to where to turn and what to do. In order to escape the shackles of paralysis, one has to consciously open their eyes and seek. A great (and necessary) rule to follow: Before you can expect others to be willing to invest in you, YOU must first be willing to invest in yourself.

While being an entrepreneur has its benefits, starting your own business is no easy task. It takes work. A lot of work. Roadblocks pop up everywhere. It is easy to be overcome with self-doubt. Being a successful entrepreneur requires a higher level of problem solving – one where many are not use to operating. Taking steps forward often begs for new creativity. And, as the great artist, Matisse, said: "Creativity takes courage."

It is my hope and my intention that The WINNING MINDSET will be a Guide that helps you to achieve your dreams sooner rather than later! While there are some "How to's" in the pages to follow, most of what I have shared focuses more on what should happen between the ears in order for you to set yourself up for greater success. I am certain that you are familiar with the old adage that one must fix oneself first before they can fix others. As an entrepreneur, you will struggle along in the process, meeting disappointment after disappointment, if your "ish" isn't right in your head. Where you are between the ears will go a long way in determining how your business grows.

The mantra for The Mobile Concierge Coaching Academy, the coaching platform that I host with my business partner, Josh Payne, reads:

COURAGE to blaze a new path
COMMITTED to a higher standard
CONFIDENCE to pursue success

Our mission is to help physical and occupational therapist break free from the standard norms of what I call "The Establishment", and lead them to the path of becoming an #uncagedclinician.

I share this in order to demonstrate my purpose of writing this book. Courage, Committed, and Confidence, are all strong, positive personality traits. These are the attributes that we want our students to develop in their quest of becoming an uncaged clinician. Yes, there are extremely important action steps that lead to growing your business. However, exhibiting Courage, being Committed, and having Confidence all start with having a Winning Mindset.

As I stated in the very beginning: Businesses are more alike than they are different. That means the principles for achieving success apply to every single freaking business out there. This is something I learned from my friend, Matt Bartlett, who owns Granite Dude – a granite countertop company in Phoenix, AZ. We have had several discussions in the past about our respective companies. In our talks, we certainly found this concept to hold true.

You may very well be a healthcare provider of some sort if you are reading this book. The discussions and stories that I share in the following chapters will apply to all who are flirting with starting out on their own; even if you are selling granite countertops. This book can also be a valuable tool for those who may be struggling with moving forward in their existing business.

I had a blast writing The Winning Mindset for the Mobile Entrepreneur. I hope you get as much enjoyment from reading it!

LET'S GOOOO!!!

1
IF YOU AIN'T FIRST, YOU'RE LAST!

One of the iconic lines from the movie "Talladega Nights", starring Will Ferrell, is "If you ain't first, you're last!" The movie is about a goofball guy who miraculously becomes a NASCAR racing champion. Ricky Bobby (Ferrell's character in the movie) would shout this to the cameras after each victory. Ricky continues to say the famous line even when his career takes a dive and he is no longer winning. We learn later in the movie that it was a line that his dad would say to him as a young boy. Of course, moviegoers thought this to be a catchy line. But, there is so much truth and value in "If you ain't first, you're last."

Before beginning on the path of entrepreneurship, you must first do a self-audit check. As my own mentor, Greg Todd, would call it: "Asset, You". In other words, you must first recognize that YOU are your biggest asset to not only starting your business, but also to growing your business. You need to have clarity in You as a person. My best friend told me something that I have gone on to share with many others: "There will never be a shortage of people to tell you what you can't do."

In moving forward as an entrepreneur, you have to recognize and expect that there will be others who do not support your dreams. They will tell you that it cannot be done. They will question if you are doing the right thing. I was having a 1:1 meeting with a young therapist, Sarah, who shared some wonderful insight. She was very happy in her new job because of the potential for advancement. Yet, she was going to be allowed to grow her on-line platform. Her ultimate goal was to not only to not be employed, but also to create a platform in which virtually all other clinicians in her field would not want to be employed either. What Sarah told me next was something that really hit the gong hard. What she said not only defined this particular chapter, but it represented the basis for this whole book: The Winning Mindset. Sarah shared that although she did not have certain credentials as of yet, she was hired for her position because of the Gift that she realized that she possessed. Furthermore, she realized her Gift ONLY AFTER setting herself straight between the ears first. When she told me this I responded that she had just summarized my entire book that I was but a few pages away from completing in literally one sentence. She recognized the first important rule: If you ain't first, you're last.

When I was applying to physical therapy schools, I was not accepted in my first year of trying. Nor was I wasn't accepted during my second year of applying. And, originally, I wasn't accepted during my third year of mailing schools application fees! Each year that I received seven to 10 letters from schools that told me "Thank you for your financial contribution to our institution. We wish you the best in your career", my father would ask me: "Well, you didn't get into school. What are you going to do now?" My answer was always: "Dad, I'm going to PT school."

During that third year of applying, I requested an interview with one program that did not grant interviews. I stated that I wanted them to base their decision on the person whom they meet; not based on some numbers on a piece of paper about a person whom they knew nothing about. Upon walking into the chairperson's office, THE VERY FIRST THING said to me was: "I do not anticipate you to get into our program, but how can I help you?" This person then proceeded to attempt to convince me to change my dreams, and that I should pursue other options.

It was at the end of my third year applying that Shenandoah University, gave me my chance. The program at Shenandoah was new, and many of their applicants feared that the school would not obtain the proper credentialing. Therefore, many students elected to attend other schools. Lucky for me, number 187 on the wait-list became number 35 in a class of 36. I was not concerned of the circumstances behind my being offered an opportunity. I was simply grateful. I knew that one day I would prevail. Why? I believed in ME. I was passionate about becoming a physical therapist. I was filled with determined grit. I was persistent. I knew deep down inside that my calling would not, could not be denied forever.

That person who was denied multiple times, and was questioned if he should continue became a physical therapist. And, guess what? I have helped thousands of people to bring the playground back into their lives. I also coach, mentor, and inspire others in the pursuit of their own dreams.

After 19 years of grinding away for others in various clinics, I started my own Mobile, cash-based physical therapy and wellness business in May 2013. Scores of people – friends, family, fellow colleagues, people in the public – told me that I HAD to take insurance if I wanted to be successful. What I found interesting was that when I mentioned my plan to my current clients in the clinic that I was going to be cash-based, not a single one told me: "Bad idea". What the naysayers did not know was that people actually WILL PAY for value. That is the reason that my clients did not question me. They knew that what I would be giving my own customers was something of a higher value on several fronts, which was a value that they were not able to receive in the clinic setting. That value was something that they knew was worth buying.

While my dad loved and supported me, he was concerned that I may be spinning my wheels. As a parent, he wanted his son to achieve success – now. Many people might be tempted to change their minds. But I knew that going to physical therapy school was my calling. I simply knew. And I did. Educational leaders suggested that I just wasn't cut out for becoming a physical therapist based on undergraduate grades. But I proved them wrong. Plenty of people told me that my plan would not work. I couldn't be successful with my idea of providing a healthcare service and expect people to pay when they could use their insurance. But I had already been exposed to a population of people who were craving this very type of service. I simply knew.

The reason that people may not support you in your dreams is that your dream is not their dream. They are not invested in what you are trying to pursue. Often times, this lack of support may be driven by the fact that they do not believe in themselves. Therefore, they try to push their own lack of faith onto you. Do not let others' limiting beliefs distract you from the belief you have in YOU.

The general population is content with being an employee. These are the "implementors" of businesses; carrying out the daily tasks being given. Implementors are needed, because as you grow your business, you are going to need implementors working for you. Some people are ok with building other's dreams. However, put yourself in a position where it is your dreams that are being built. That is one reason why you are reading this book!

Being first and not last is more than just drowning out the doubters and haters to focus on the belief you have in you. It is important to recognize – and own- the fact that your success moving forward is dependent on no one other than you. You being First addresses the fact that it is imperative that you identify both your strengths and your weaknesses in order to achieve the success that you seek. Growing a business is about taking your customer to a higher level. Knowing your strengths, and implementing them, will take your customer to the next level – a level in which they desire. It is equally important to be self-aware of your weaknesses in order for your business to continue upward growth. Working on your weaknesses will help your business to grow. Impacting lives has everything to do with moving people forward from their current situation. You must be able to take steps forward in your business before you, as a business, can move people – your customers - forward.

Achieving success, being First, has a lot to do with how you perceive yourself – and how others perceive you. How you perceive yourself has a lot to do with the thoughts that are going on between the ears. The more that you are self-aware, then the more confident you will be in yourself and in what you are doing. The public, and your customers, will feel that confidence. And, as we all know, Confidence sells.

I mentioned earlier the four things that ultimately lead to my physical therapy school acceptance: belief, passion, grit, and persistence. These four attributes are imperative for anyone who journeys into entrepreneurship for I wholeheartedly believe (no pun intended) that these are the four foundational pillars to a thriving business.

Having self-awareness includes true, genuine Belief not only in you, but also in what it is you are pursuing. My dream of becoming a physical therapist would not have come true if I did not believe in myself, and have belief that physical therapy was my calling. Additionally, had I lacked belief in me, I would have caved to the naysayers and doubters. Fast-forward 19 years. If I did not fully believe in me, then Bayliff Integrated Wellness might not have survived the first two years of being scared sh##less every day.

Closely tied into Belief is Passion. The business you are contemplating should be something for which you have true Passion. It is much easier to sell something that you feel a deep connection towards. Passion for something also feeds into the confidence you have regarding that "thing". As I have already stated: Confidence sells. I am going to address this a little more in the next chapter.

Being an entrepreneur and running a business definitely has its sex appeal. When you build your dreams, you have a better opportunity at living the life you desire. But getting there is not easy. It takes work. Hard work. It takes Grit. There are two main reasons why businesses fail (outside of being a restaurant with terrible food). Reason #1: the people simply don't know that you exist. Gaining a presence takes Grit. I am going to speak to this more in the next chapter.

The second reason why businesses fail is that the person (you) simply decided to quit. Persistence is so important for many reasons. Do not fall for the mantra established by the hit movie FIELD OF DREAMS: "Build it, and they will come". Simply opening your doors will not cause the phone to ring and people to walk in. Building a business is like growing a tree, a rose bush, or any other plant – you have to feed it and water it, feed it and water it, feed it and water it. Think about the best barbeque or steak you have ever tasted. The restaurant let that meat marinate for 24 to 36 hours. You must give your business time to marinate. Doing so requires persistence in watering it and feeding it. Again, had I not been persistent in my endeavors of attending graduate school, then chances are you are not reading this book right now. I had a friend several years ago – actually at the same time I was starting my business – that had grown tired of the corporate world. He decided to obtain his real estate license. Meanwhile, he took a position with a startup company selling "green lighting". He quickly found his first potential homebuyer; however, they just couldn't decide on a property. With the green lighting company, he was in negotiations with a very popular athletic company that was interested in the product. But, again, they were not making their choice quickly. Frustrated at the inability to close a deal, my friend found himself back in the corporate world after only eight months. Care to guess what happened once he quit his own dreams? That's right. The couple called to say they had made a decision, and the athletic company phoned to say: "we are ready to buy!"

Be persistent.

While starting a business can be daunting and scary, doing so can be a lot easier than you might think. But, I am not going to sugar

7

coat it. It does take work, which is much more enjoyable and easier to swallow when the work you are doing is directly for you and your family. There are steps that you need to follow in order to reach where it is you want to be. I'll address this more in the following chapters. The first step is to recognize that if you ain't first, you're last.

TAKE HOME POINTS

- Develop self-awareness
- Identify your strengths and weaknesses
- There will never be a shortage of people to tell you what you can't do
- Your dreams are not others' dreams
- YOU are your greatest weapon

2
THE FOUR CORNERS

Back in the mid to late 1970's, the late Dean Smith, Hall of Fame Basketball coach of the University of North Carolina Tar Heels, was the mastermind of an offensive play called "The Four Corners". Coach Smith would direct his team to execute the Four Corners late in a game when victory seemed at hand. Very often this ploy would work because there was no shot clock in play. In fact, today's college basketball world can thank Coach Dean Smith for causing the revolution for a shot clock.

During the Four Corners, a member of the team would stand in each corner of the offensive half of the court. Meanwhile, the point guard (at the time, Phil Ford) would dribble all around the court; occasionally passing the ball to one of his teammates standing in a corner. He would then retrieve the ball and proceed to dribble around the court. You may be wondering: "How does this apply to me?"

Before starting a business, there are four questions that you must first answer. Like the point guard (Phil Ford), you are going to have to address each question with some deep thought. Answering each one to the fullest will help you to gain the victory. that is at hand. In fact, there are going to be more questions in later chapters that I will discuss that will require you to dive deep into answering them. It is the only sure-fire way to a) gain success sooner, rather than later; b) to attract the type of customer that you want.

PASSION

I can still recall as if it were yesterday the moment that I declared that being a physical therapist was what I was determined to do in life. During the summer of 1987, after my junior year at Wake Forest University, I volunteered at the only physical therapy clinic in the entire county where I lived, Stewart Physical Therapy. I knew Ed Stewart, the owner. His son and I played tennis at the same club. Additionally, I knew another therapist in the clinic, who was also a member of the same racquet club. Mr. Stewart was more than delighted when I called and offered free labor for the summer! You can imagine that with his clinic being the only one for an entire county that he was quite busy.

This was my first-time having work exposure to a business other than the part-time summer jobs I had previously at the racquet club. The clinic was filled with people who were facing various challenges – pain, limitations from surgery, recovering from a stroke, etc. I marveled at how the therapists made each person laugh; taking them away from their challenges if but for an hour or so. It was also truly amazing to watch someone overcome their deficits and regain the life they once had. The looks on their faces were simply priceless.

The giving of Hope and Inspiration that were involved as a person was taken through his or her transformation resonated with my inner soul. Coaching, encouraging and helping others to achieve, were things that I recognized long before that I truly enjoyed. Physical Therapy was an avenue in which I could blend the coaching, the encouraging, and the helping along with my love of sport and physical activity to take people on a journey that would mean so much more to them in their lives. As I pulled out of my parking spot at the end of my second day at Stewart's, I paused in my blue 2-door Honda Accord. Giving the clinic a long glance, I pointed to the door and said out loud: "THAT is what I am going to do in life."

In chapter one I mentioned that one of the key pillars to achieving success was to know that the profession you are pursuing is your Passion. Venturing into your own business should be towards something that you love – for many reasons. Soon after the inception of Bayliff Integrated Wellness, I was asked by a chiropractor why I left the clinic setting to begin a mobile cash-based practice. I was able to answer nearly before he finished his question: "Because I love what I do."

Answering the Passion question is more than "what do you love to do?" You may love (hopefully) being a therapist, or a dentist, or a granite counter-top installer, or a dog groomer, or... whatever, but there is more that goes into the Passion of what do you love to do. I will address this in a later chapter.

PROBLEM

In chapter one I talked about having self-awareness of your strengths and weaknesses in order to move forward in your business, and to move your customers forward. The best way, and possibly the only way, to advance not only yourself, but also your customers, is that you must identify what problems are out there. Knowing and understanding the problems that your potential customers face will go a long way in the message that you develop; in how you market; and in how you serve as a guide for your customers. When you identify problems, you create opportunities for moving your customers forward. Questions to dive into regarding your potential customer will be discussed in a later chapter.

It is equally important to identify your own problems – i.e. having self-awareness – in order to avoid struggling with achieving success in your business. You are not going to have all the answers. You are not going to know how to perform every start-up detail. So, you must be willing to be resourceful in problem solving. Seek out the guidance of others whose strengths are your weaknesses.

I have had many ideas that I wanted to pursue for quite some time. The problem was that I was clueless as to where to begin. I also recognized that I had trouble "selling" despite my strength in developing relationships. I knew that in order to move towards my goal of time freedom, I had to "level myself up". I owned up to the fact that I did not have all the know-how or skill. So, I turned to my now coach, Greg Todd. In fact, I currently have four coaches to guide me through various aspects of my business goals. I had to accept the fact that until I moved myself forward, I was going to continue to struggle with two important things in my business: a) moving others forward; b) more importantly, attracting customers TO move forward.

You are always going to run into problems for both yourself, and for your customer. The beauty in this is that identifying problems offers opportunities to taking steps forward. Solving problems should be at the core of what you do in business. Identify problems, find solutions, and your business will grow.

PRESENCE

You can probably state the three most important rules in real estate, and for every single business out there: "Location. Location. Location." Where your business sits can have a huge impact on your success. I mentioned in the first chapter that one of the main reasons that a business fails are that people simply do not know that the business exists. "Build it, and they will come" just isn't so. Build it, yes. But the public must know that you are out there. You can be the best damn whatever in town, but if you are quiet, no one is going to find you.

If you are developing a brick-and-mortar business, then you probably can understand the Location concept. So, how does this apply to someone starting a mobile service? The answer for them goes for the brick-and-mortar, also! Yes, presence also speaks to where happen to be so that people see you. But the physical location is more than a busy street corner. Presence includes where you are informing the public that you have solutions to their problems. In today's world, if you are a successful businessperson, chances are you also have a strong social media presence. You may not personally be "the face" of your social media campaigns, but your business has a presence. Having a presence also means that you are seen in various venues, at other businesses, events, and meetings. I will speak more to this later. For now, understand that the purpose of presence is to establish you and your business as the authority, the expert, and the go-to.

PROFIT

My wife is a schoolteacher. She is beyond passionate about organization. She thrives on designing her classroom. Helping other teachers with organization and design is something that she would absolutely love to do. But, there is just one little problem. Primary (and secondary) schoolteachers do not earn viable wages. This is an unfortunate issue that others are free to discuss outside of this book. But the fact is, teachers don't make money. I can say that because my wife is a teacher. And, trust me, she isn't compensated enough for the work she does. It is no secret that teachers are required to pay for their own classroom supplies with their own money – money that they do not make. There are plenty of free resources that teachers can refer to for classroom ideas. Why should a struggling teacher pay for a service that they can obtain for free through any number of resources? The point is, you may have a passion for something, but is it profitable? Let's be honest here. Unless you have been lucky enough to have had your favorite six numbers come up, you are not going into business to offer your services for free.

If you are a healthcare provider, perhaps your passion is to serve an audience that may be considered underprivileged. Or, due to the economics of your community, the town residents are simply on the lower spectrum of the socio-economic status. If either is the case, it does not mean that serving them will be impossible. But it does affect your business model.

There are some situations where your audience cannot afford to pay, regardless of how fantastic the value may be. In such instances, offering only cash-based services probably does not make the best business sense. Therefore, your business model may need to be an insurance-based practice. The audience can still be a profitable one. But the model shifts. Here, I identified a problem not only for (you), but also for (your) customer. Having self-awareness of the conflict allowed for the two coinciding problems to then be solved.

If you are thinking about starting your own business, regardless of what the business entails, you are doing so for several reasons. I will get to this later. In order to meet your true goals of having your own business, you are going to have to make money. Do not apologize for wanting to make money, especially to yourself.

Now you have given deep thought to the "Four Corners". If you recall the story of the UNC Tar Heels, that Phil Ford was running the show. Much like Ford, you must be the point guard of your business; particularly in getting started through answering these questions. What does this look like? The point guard (Ford) knew where to go to get to each corner. In other words, he knew the Pathway. You must know the pathway to finding your clients. Where are they? Where do they hang out on social media? How do they like to be communicated to? You are the point guard, the star player; the Go-To person. Know your pathway to reaching your clients so that they know who you are.

REVIEW OF "FOUR CORNERS"

When thinking about embarking on your own dreams, answer these four questions:

1. What are you Passionate about?
2. What are the Problems that exist?
3. How can you gain a Presence?
4. Is this Profitable?

You are the Point Guard in the Four Corners. Know your Pathway to not only finding your clients, but the pathway for your clients to find you.

3
THE MORAL OF YOUR STORY

You have undoubtedly heard a thousand times, if not fifty times, "What is your WHY?" This is the first question that people are asked to answer when they are looking to embark on their entrepreneurial journey. Not only is it a great question, the answer is also the foundational rock for pursuing one's dreams.

It is very common that when I ask my coaching students to identify their WHY, they respond with "I want to treat clients the way I want to treat. And I want to be able to give them the care that they deserve." However, they are perplexed when I tell them that their answer is their WHAT.

Free tip #3: Every therapist who is contemplating starting their own practice chooses to do so because they want to treat clients the way they want to treat.

I correlate this answer as to the modern-day Wheel of Fortune. When the game show first aired, all of the contestants would immediately guess the letters R, S, T, L, and N. Since every contestant guessed these letters first, the show decided to automatically give the players these letters. Thereby, essentially telling them to think again. To say that you want to treat the way you want is like the R, S, T, L, and N. Think harder.

Don't get me wrong. Treating the way you want is a FANTAWESOME reason to do your own thing. But to treat the way you want is more of the vehicle that allows you to build your dreams. It is a WHAT. Physical Therapy, Occupational Therapy, and all other healthcare professions are tools used to perform the "what" that leads to living the "why". Your WHY is something – or, should be something – that is on a deeper level. The WHY is the Moral of Your Story.

When I suggest for one to go deeper into their Why, what I am asking them to do is to figure out their bottom line. At the end of the day, what is all of this for? What is it that they truly want?

What is the moral of their story? Knowing this is so important because the Why gives your What purpose and meaning. A Why that is well understood enables one to pursue their What with passion.

I watched a video of the motivational speaker, Michael J. He asked a member of the audience what he did as a profession. The gentleman responded that he was a music teacher. Michael J asked the person if he could sing a couple of verses of "Amazing Grace". The teacher complied. He sang "Amazing Grace" with a deep, rich voice worthy of the song. He was phenomenal. After Michael J praised him for his talent (which was astounding), he created a scenario for the music teacher. He said: "Imagine this. Imagine that your uncle had been shot running from a crime. He was hospitalized and placed in jail. Now, your uncle is being released. He is set free, free to come home. Now, sing Amazing Grace."

The raw power and emotion that then flowed out of this man was nothing short of Spiritual. Notes were held longer. The voice hit a deeper range. The man's soul could be felt on the listener's skin as chill bumps rose. The music teacher was close to tears as he sang. The audience was in tears. Michael J was in tears. And, heck, I was a blubbering fool watching this miracle on video. The man undoubtedly received a standing ovation. And to that, Michael J told the man, and the audience, that what they had just heard and witnessed was the man's Why. Teaching music was merely his what. The deep, Spiritual Why gave his What purpose.

Identifying your true Why also serves as motivation to taking a step forward every day. This is so important because there will be days when you feel as though you just can't take a step. Some days will be met with what feels like an unbeatable struggle. There will be rejections and objections that seem to come like rapid-fire. Anticipated results will not go as planned. You will stare into the faces of frustration and self-doubt. In that moment of fight or flight, you will be in a battle with yourself to resist the urge to quit.

A rock-solid Why strengthens your Belief. It breathes life into your Passion. It empowers you with Grit. All of these enable you to continue to take a step forward. Thus, it charges your Persistence. Belief, Passion, Grit, Persistence. Do these sound familiar? Your WHY is a description of how you want your personal and professional life to look. Your WHAT allows you to live that Life.

For you, your Why may be something such as to create time freedom for yourself and your family. Your Why may be to escape financial struggles. Perhaps your Why is on a more Spiritual level. At the end of the day, what is it that is going to be of most importance to you. One of my student's WHY's was to be able to purchase a home for her and her son. I have talked to many people who tell me that they want to be able to make it to their children's little league games. This is a bit on the humorous side, but for nearly 19 years I joked that I did not know what this concept of "Happy Hour" meant. Now, being able to go to Happy Hour may not be the strongest of WHY's. If it is your WHY, well... I'm not judging. The story of the music teacher singing Amazing Grace was a story of God. I respect that not everyone has a relationship with God, or a god. But I will promise you this. Regardless of your beliefs, there IS SOMETHING for each and every person that makes him or her stop and say: "This. THIS is why, right here." You may very much so want to treat clients the way you want to treat clients. In doing so, what does that do for you personally? For your family? For your children? At the very end of the day, what is it that you really and truly want?

Hopefully now you can see now that the R, S, T, L, and N are nothing more than puzzle pieces that you need in order to achieve the answer that you desire.

Take Home Points

- At the end of the day, what is it that you truly want? How is it that you want your life to look?
- Your WHY gives your WHAT purpose and meaning.
- Your WHY is the solid foundation for the sole purpose for which you are pursuing your dreams

4
YOU NEED TO THINK ABOUT WHAT YOU'RE DOING

Since this is my book, and I can name things as I want, I'm calling this chapter: "YOU NEED TO THINK ABOUT WHAT YOU'RE DOING". This is something that I have heard from my father a million times. Dad, thank you for helping me with a chapter title! For you, the reader, what in the heck am I talking about? Simple: MINDSET. But to title this "Mindset" seemed too... boring. Let's have fun here; maybe even a chuckle.

So much of this chapter goes back to chapter one: "If You're Ain't First, You're Last". As I work through this you see that having that self-awareness is going to go a long way in how you begin your journey. "Think about what you're doing", aka "Mindset", is vital to so many elements as you take steps forward. Having the right Mindset will not only help in your business' growth, but it will also help you to avoid many internal roadblocks and pitfalls. Trust me. I have been able to eliminate a good deal of stress simply by adopting the right frame of mind. If I didn't, I would have a lot more gray hair – or less, all together!

There have been scores of books written on, and a myriad of podcasts devoted to Mindset. Since not everyone reads development books or listens to podcasts, I'm going to address this. Which, by the way, THANK YOU for choosing to read this one! Even for those who are astutely aware of MINDSET, this will still be a great reminder!

As I mentioned, my father would say to me: "You need to think about what you're doing" whenever I would do something that, perhaps, could have used a little more thought. It's the giving more thought to things that I want to emphasize here. There are two general types of Mindsets: Growth and Closed. Which are you?

CLOSED MINDSET

I first want to acknowledge that there are a lot of business owners who, in my opinion, have a closed mindset; yet they are quite successful. O.K. There. I guess right off the bat, being closed minded is not such a big deal.

What exactly is a Closed Mindset? In general, having a closed mindset means several things. Being closed-minded implies that you are not open to opportunities. These individuals are going along their path totally unreceptive to directions and suggestions, even if they happen to be going the wrong way. This is different from following your dream and your mission. One who is closed-minded may not be willing to hear what could make their mission get more recognition. Their dream may garner an even larger impact if they made a tweak here and there. "Come Hell or High Water", their way is The Way.

A closed mindset also limits one in the opportunities that they can create. It puts the breaks on moving forward because one can have the tendency to easily say it can't be done, or it has already been done. If this is you, well, let me be blunt about two things: a) thank you for purchasing my book; b) you might as well turn back now, because what you are wanting to build has already been built by someone else. In fact, I am willing to guess that what you want to build has already been built by a host of others. So, if you think you cannot do it, then you are right. I can promise you that the leaders of Wendy's and Burger King did not sit in their board rooms thinking: "Well, crap. McDonald's beat us to it."

Business owners who are closed-minded also tend to look at their respective market as what has been eloquently described by others as a "red ocean". In this frame of mind, one sees everyone else in the industry as competition. Vying for customers is a dog-eat-dog world. Everyone is scrambling for table scraps. They sense that they are faced with having to fight for an already limited client base. Many entrepreneurs may even feel that there is no way that they can compete with the larger businesses. But as I will discuss in a moment, you can.

OPEN MINDSET

The beautiful thing about an Open Mindset is that it frees one's thinking to allow for opportunities to be seen as "Win-Win" situations. Better yet, an Open Mindset means that a person not only SEES everything AS an opportunity; but one also SEEKS OUT opportunities. With this outlook, the world is a "blue ocean" – there are opportunities everywhere with plenty to go around. In the most simplistic form, one who possess an open mindset one does not look at others as the competition.

In the beginning of the previous section, CLOSED MINDSET, I mentioned that I know business owners who hold their cards tight to their chest.

They look at others who do the same thing as they do as the competition. I was even told that the clinic director of my last place of employment considered me – a cash-based solopreneur – as the competition to his multi-therapist clinic that accepted all insurances! I even know others who provide mobile services who do not share any information about their practice or referral sources. They speak only of how many visits per week they are seeing. And, yes, these individuals are all finding success and are seeing their businesses grow.

What these owners fail to embrace (and fully accept) is that in a city of over 2 million people, they cannot possibly serve everyone. Scottsdale, alone, has a population of 250,000, which swells from October to May. There are plenty of people who need servicing. Unfortunately (or fortunately for me), Closed Minded business owners look at attracting clients as vying for table scraps. They see a red ocean.

Let's go back to chapter one for a moment. This is where I talked about having self-awareness. An Open Mindset requires one to have such strong self-awareness that one is able to see, and to OWN, that they have a UNIQUE GIFT to share with the world. When one recognizes and owns that they possess a Unique Value Proposition (UVP), then there is no competition. This is the very reason that Burger King, Wendy's, and a plethora of boutique hamburger joints thrive amongst the ever-present McDonalds. And why do the boutique hamburger restaurants win despite charging more for a burger and fries than the fast-food chains? It is because they have their own UVP's. And why does one burger joint (examples in my town: HOPDODDY, SMASH BURGER, LUSH BURGER, ZIN BURGER) attract clientele over another? It is because each has created their UVP. I ask this: did each of these restaurants hold back on their dreams because the idea had already been done? Or... did each recognize that there were plenty of people out there who are hungry? They also asked themselves: "What problem do we want to solve?". Hmmm... Does that sound familiar? What problem is there to solve?

What is your Unique Value Proposition? This can be a number of things. But at the end of the day, it boils down to who YOU are as a person. Your UVP is defined by the Gift that you have to give. If you have the talent of putting people at ease and brightening their day, that may be your UVP that attracts people to you. Perhaps you were a collegiate runner and you continue to participate in organized runs. You probably then are able to connect with other runners through your experience. You understand their mindset, their fears, what drives them. THAT is your Gift, your UVP, which sets you apart and draws the runner to you. It may very well be your Empathy that you have for those suffering from chronic pain. These individuals are often accustomed to being shifted off from one provider to the next;

each unsure as to what to do. Your empathy and listening skills are your Gift to the chronic pain sufferers, which allows them to connect with you. Better yet, they form a trust in you.

A person who embodies a growth mindset and embraces opportunities is also one who is willing to seek growth in oneself. I can promise you this: If you do not actively pursue growth in you or your business, then you will start to decline. Your business is likely to suffer a slow death. My high school tennis coach use to say to us, with regards to practice: "You either get better, or you get worse. But you never stay the same." I have heard that in my head for over 35 years now.

Embracing growth means that one is willing to suffer a bit and to get uncomfortable in order to win. A great story that I heard from an amazing business coach, Myron Golden, is one of a seed. He spoke about a seed becoming a tree. He used a drawing board to help illustrate his point. He had already talked about things going down or going in reverse before pushing upward or outward. So, as he asked the question of the seed and was ready to draw on the board, everyone shouted: "It must grow roots down into the ground!" To this, Myron answered: "No!" We all sat a little perplexed. Did he not just say how things go down before going up? What Myron followed with was absolutely... Golden. Pun, intended.

While we all thought that the answer was the seed must first start to grow roots down into the ground before bursting up through the soil, Myron pointed out that in order for a seed to become a tree it must first make the decision to cease being a seed. BOOM. How simple. How brilliant.

I am certain that many of you would argue that a seed really is not able to make a conscious decision to do something since it does not possess a brain. But, you get the point. In order to become that which you were meant to be, you must first make the decision to no longer live in your current comfortable state. Here is a free tip: No one has ever achieved at ANYTHING because they remained comfortable. Steve Jobs, Bill Gates, Beyoncé, Garth Brooks, Michael Jordan, LeBron James, Tom Brady, Roger Federer, Serena Williams, Tiger Woods, etc. etc. achieved because they got very uncomfortable with busting their arses; pushing themselves; working on something that they lacked that was preventing them from making it to the top.

In my own practice, I had to learn to get comfortable with answering the question: "Do you take my insurance?" I will admit that I dreaded answering this question. I would fumble over my words. This certainly did not convey any measure of confidence. More often than not, I was unsuccessful in my attempt to convince the person on the phone that it was in their best interest to pay me rather than go elsewhere and receive treatment with the false pretense that they were getting it for free. I had to challenge myself to learn a dialogue that would give me the opportunity to succeed in that situation.

A more uncomfortable situation that I had to challenge myself with – and one to which many of you can relate – was simply the decision to leave a known, steady paycheck. I had to be willing to leave a job where all I had to do was show up, work long hours, and I was sure to be paid a salary and receive benefits. But having a job did not allow me to grow the life that I had always envisioned having one day. Rather than my salaried job giving me security, it was causing me to go in the wrong direction financially. Overworked and Underpaid. Sound familiar?

Here is free tip #2: No one has ever achieved the life they truly desire with a paycheck. Certainly not when you are at the "staff level".

An important quality that one with a Growth/Abundance Mindset has is that of Gratitude. These individuals tend to be grateful for the opportunities that they create. Yes, create. Things "come your way" because you created the environment for the opportunity to present itself. Having gratitude means that one is willing to give back before asking for anything any return. Often times, one gives with no intention of receiving. This can be demonstrated in many ways. One example would be giving of one's time to provide free screenings at a local venue (YMCA, golf club, running club, etc.) without the expectation of getting any referrals in return. In fact, the screenings are provided with no intention of trying to sell one's own services. Something that I have done is to write an occasional article for a physician's newsletter. I offered her patients free health information with no mention of "Call me if you want to know more!" In the private Facebook group I own, The Mobile PT League, I share my knowledge (KNAHLEDGE, I like to say) with the group on a weekly basis. I did so for well over a year before I ever asked for anything in return – the release of my business coaching program. I continue to share information in the group each week. Even on my own personal Facebook page, I give away free health tips every Thursday – Thirsty Thursday – where we Thirst for Knahledge! I do this for two reasons: 1) because I like doing it. Well, let's be real. I LOVE doing it. 2) it is a way for me to serve many people at once. And, guess what, I have obtained clients from these LIVES. They reached out to me NOT because I asked, but because I gave and they developed a trust in me.

Achieving success is not about squeezing every penny out of every individual. There is a lot of Karma that coincides with finding success. What many fail to understand is that in order to receive, one must first give; and give a lot. Giving builds trust. Gratitude is a much greater attractor than selfishness or ego.

Take Home Points

- Growth Mindset/ Abundance Mindset/ seeks opportunities and recognizes that opportunities are everywhere.
- Through Abundance, there is plenty to go around. There is no competition.
- Showing Gratitude and Serving is a Winning Attitude
- Fixed Mindset/Closed Mindset sees everyone else as competition.
- Closed Mindset is not open to possibilities or options

5
THIS IS NOTHING

"Zeus" was a teammate on my high school tennis team. The dude was blessed with height (6'2"), quickness, ridiculous eye-hand coordination, and the strength of an ox. He could take the life out of a hard-hit ball and send it back only to have it rest gently on the court. Retrieving the shot was impossible. He also could pound the living daylights out of a shot so strongly that, well, I think I still have a bruise from one of his hits 40 years later. He could hang with anybody on the court. He eventually received a tennis scholarship from one of the top collegiate tennis programs at the time.

Unfortunately, Zeus never reached his potential. He could have played higher on his university's team. He could have made All-American. He had all the talent in the world to have played the sport on television. But those things never happened.

I firmly believe that the only thing that held Zeus back from making a living playing tennis is that he failed to recognize the importance of owning his Gift. So many of us would state with frustration: "As hard as we train, if we had his talent, we would be playing pro!" Zeus simply failed to own his Gift. Actually, his downfall was that he knew he was gifted; he just didn't fully embrace it.

However, for many of us, we are unable to recognize that we possess a Gift. We fail to acknowledge our Gift because it comes so natural to us. Zeus had God-given talent. It was natural for him to be supernatural on the court. Therefore, he was unable to achieve his potential.

Many of us resort to self-deprivation when complemented, or simply, when speaking of ourselves. The reason is that the "thing" that we do that draws praise and attention from others comes so naturally to us, that we do not view it as anything special. We think that we should feel good for only of the things for which we have worked hard to develop and/or to achieve. What we often fail to recognize is that it is those things that we do so effortlessly that others appreciate. It is these things that inspire others to want to undergo some form of transformation, regardless of how big or small. Andy Warhol was quoted as saying: "Everything has its beauty; not everyone sees it." Unfortunately, it is the beauty in ourselves that we far too often miss.

There are four major points to the importance of owning your Gift.

CONFIDENCE in SELF

One of the things that I do well is to develop relationships with people. I do this with endless encouragement. When others doubt their own talent, I am able to show them something that they have done that has made a huge impact on people – example(s) that THEY are able to acknowledge. So often I receive compliments for my ability to lift up others. I discredited such kindness for far too long. As I grew, I learned to accept the fact that I DO offer inspiration to others. As I began to accept this, I became more confident in myself. I learned to speak positively in my own head to the most important person in the world: me. The brain is a powerful beast. Feed it words, and those words become thoughts. Repeated thoughts become actions. Actions lead to beliefs.

Helpful tip#5: You are going to go a lot further with believing in the outcome that you desire, rather than expecting the outcome that you want to avoid.

Hopefully, by now you are starting to see why chapter 1 was Chapter 1.

CONFIDENCE FROM OTHERS

If there is one attribute that people seek in others, it is CONFIDENCE. How often have you not purchased something simply because the person sharing information with you seemed unsure of the information themselves? How awkward is it to sit in a presentation in which the presenter is timid; language is used that suggests that they are not fully trusting of what they are sharing? Chances are greater that you did NOT buy from the person – unless you really, really wanted the product no matter what. I'm guessing that you would leave the lecture with doubt and questions. When you have confidence in YOU, others will feel that confidence resulting in you being recognized as an authority, a leader, and a go-to person.

DEVELOPS A CONNECTION & TRUST

The happy snowball effect continues in motion. As your confidence builds within you, others feel that confidence and they look to you as a leader. Once you viewed as a leader and an authority, you now develop a connection with people. They "get" what you are saying. They thirst for more. Internally, they begin to trust you. Buying from you now becomes a much easier decision for them to make.

YOUR GIFT IS YOUR ASSET

Your Gift, or your Unique Value Proposition (UVP) is the single biggest attractor for people to you. Is your Gift for everyone? Not hardly, because people are different. But there are plenty of people out there who are not only looking for your Gift, but they are also craving it. Use your Gift to attract those customers. Depending on your business, it does not take a lot of customers. It just takes the right customers. Your Gift will attract the right customers for you.

Review of the Importance of Owning Your Gift

- Helps to instill Confidence in You
- Instills Confidence felt from your customer
- Develops Connection and Trust
- Your Gift IS your asset

6
YOU MUST BECOME YOUR FIRST CUSTOMER

One of the first questions that people ask when they are starting their own business is "How do I get clients?" I have even been asked this question before the person has even business-sized themselves. This is the $1M question, indeed. While there are a lot of things that go into acquiring clients, the first thing that you must do to attract your clients is that you must become your first customer.

Several elements are in play here. Before expecting anyone to invest in you, you must invest in YOU first. You cannot expect to take people to a higher level if you have not taken yourself to a higher level, plain and simple. One way to do this is by finding a paid coach or mentor. Yes, paid. Why paid? When you pay someone to do something as simple as hold you accountable, you are ten times more likely to perform the task even if you already know the information. Why? Because you have spent hard earned money to have someone to tell you to quit kicking tires and do something. It's just fact.

Tip #4: Rarely has anyone ever made a drastic change in life or business from free advice.

While I am on the subject of investing, I am going to go on a brief A.D.D. tangent. But it has relevance to you being your first customer. Later on in the book I will talk about energy, but I want to speak of a particular energy now. If you expect others to spend money on you, then nurture Karma by spending a little money yourself. I find it interesting the number of people I encounter – therapists, or otherwise – who command top dollar for their services in their businesses. They become baffled and frustrated when the public balks at their prices. Yet, in their own personal affairs, they consistently seek out the cheapest price on goods. Now, don't get me wrong. I like to save money just as much as the next person. This is just something that I have observed. I like to believe in Karma. In my experience, I feel as though what I put out comes back to me.

40

Acquiring clients, getting people to buy into what it is you are selling, can also be broken down into a four-step process; one that starts with YOU. I call this the 4 D's to someone saying: "I would love to give you money!" - Dive, Discover, Delight, Delegate.

DIVE

As I have already stated, before taking any one to the next level, you must first take yourself to the next level. How do you do this? By DIVING into the topic yourself. Whatever it is that you wish to offer to people, you must Dive into the subject. Live it. Breathe it. BE it. Openly talk about what your Mission is with people, regardless of whether or not they are your potential customers. Actively seek resources on the subject. If there are processes that you plan on teaching, perform the processes yourself. This may even include learning effective ways to communicate your knowledge, or strategies to help others to overcoming self-limiting beliefs. Diving into the subject also means involving yourself with the people. This may be through activities like workshops, blogs, publishing articles in newsletters, etc. Diving also includes activities such as listening to a number of podcasts, reading others' blog, and so forth. Diving comes down to one simple thing: Do you BELIEVE in what it is you are doing? It has to start here. Sound familiar? It is so vital that you believe in you first. Only then can you believe in your mission. And only then will the people have any belief in you. Remember: If you ain't first, your last.

DISCOVER

Closely associated with Diving is to DISCOVER as much as possible about the topic. In other words, learn everything you can as it relates to you selling your product or service. Again, while it would be a good idea to be rather astute in the subject of what you are selling to others – i.e. the journey that you are wanting to take them through - it is equally important that you learn HOW to effectively communicate to others in order to help them to see the value in what it is you are selling.

You are also going to be taking your clients and potential clients on a discovery mission, which you must lead. Your audience must view you as a leader, or they will not buy.

DELIGHT

My favorite classes in high school were all three of my Spanish classes. Learning a language that was completely foreign to me (no pun intended) was thrilling. I found that studying Spanish actually took me on a journey away from the everyday. It took me to a different place; a New World. I engulfed the language with passion. My classmates would all listen intently when it was my turn to recite dialogues given as homework. They marveled at how fluently I trilled my R's. Somehow, I was able to shape my lazy Southern mouth in a way that enabled me to properly pronounce each vowel. I probably take more pride in the fact that I finished each year in Spanish with the highest grade – the first time that happened in the history of the school – than I did in making straight A's through high school.

Dr. Steven Tepper was my advisor and one of my professors during graduate school. I absolutely loved his classes. The cardio-pulmonary information he taught may not have always come easy to me, but I loved his class. Dr. Tepper lectured with picture slides. Undoubtedly, there were always 2-3 random slides in the presentation that had absolutely nothing to do with the lecture. When they popped up, Dr. Tepper would tell the class a story about the picture; which usually involved a wild time. My favorite involved the story of going backwards over a rapid during one of his white-water rafting trips, all the while mooning the camera that took pictures of the rafters.

The common theme between the two is that both situations involved Fun. There was Delight. I studied Spanish intensely because I loved it. I envisioned myself living in another country communicating to a community where others could not. I made learning Spanish not boring. The same is true for my cardio-pulmonary class in graduate school. Dr. Tepper made the class not boring. He delighted us with stories. He cracked jokes. He made us laugh.

Bottom line is that you NEED to make the process fun; both for yourself and for the customer. Whether you are attracting leads, converting leads, or taking customers on their journeys, you will have much more success if you Delight the audience. In other words, make it entertaining.

DELEGATE

The final step in getting your customer to say: "Yes" to you – i.e. to buy from you – is to give them an action step. One effective way is to share a story, or stories, of other's success with your product or service. The customer (potential customer) needs not only to understand that what you have to offer is in their best interest, but they need to believe that your offer is in their best interest. Telling a story helps them to see this.

Once you have told your story and shared with your audience why your product or service is the right choice for them, it is important that you give your audience the opportunity to take the next steps with you in the transformation that they are seeking. You must Delegate an opportunity to them. People act when they feel empowered. Make sure you have made your audience feel this way.

Recap of getting your audience to say "Yes" to you

- You must say "Yes" to YOU first
- Dive into the subject. Become obsessed
- Discover everything about the topic for yourself, and for your audience
- Delight. Make the journey FUN for you and for your audience
- Delegate by giving your audience an action step to do the darn thing

7
ROGER FEDERER

I spent the first half of my life on a tennis court. Summers were spent traveling all over North Carolina and South Carolina, even into Georgia, to play tournaments. I had the good fortune to play on the college level as a walk-on at Wake Forest University. Back then if I went more than a day without stepping onto the court, I would go through withdrawals. I was no different than an addict. I would get antsy. I would look longingly at a tennis court whenever I drove past one in the car. I actually still do that today, despite not getting to hit as often as I would like.

For me, Roger Federer is simply The GOAT. The Greatest of All Time in tennis. He moves (verb in the present tense, because as I write this he is still playing on the ATP tour) as effortlessly and as gracefully as the best male ballerina ever: Mikhail Baryshnikov. When asked about the amazing shots that he hit in a match, he answers with: "(my opponent) forced me to have to hit that." When he loses, he gives no excuses. He lost because his opponent beat him.

If given the opportunity, I would work with Roger Federer for free – particularly if money were no issue. Does that mean I have a man-crush on Roger? Well, maybe. But that is not why I would work with Roger. I would work with Roger because tennis is something that I know quite well.

I understand the game. I understand the language. I know what goes on inside the tennis player's mind. I know what it takes to compete at a high level. And I can tell you that to get there is a grind – a very long and hard grind. I recognize what is at stake for them, and the fears they may have. I know what being successful means to their career. I get what winning and losing both do to their ego. When a player has a particular injury, I can rehab the injury with a keen understanding of what that player needs to be able to do physically. Shortly put, I am able to check off the "Four D's" to having a tennis player commit to a "Yes" to me.

Roger Federer is my Avatar.

The second major step in the Entrepreneurial Journey is identifying your Avatar. Who, or, what is your Avatar? Several factors go into deciding this. The easiest one is who would you work with for free if money were no object?

As I described above, I know a thing or two about tennis. But does that mean that you must know all the ins and outs of a sport if you are choosing to work with a particular athlete? No, not necessarily. But it would certainly help if you could at least speak the language. Why? Because, like it or not, image is everything. When choosing to work with a group of individuals, you must know SOMETHING associated with the group in order to gain their trust. Remember: business success is built on relationships, which spawn from trust. Additionally, when there is a level of passion for the person you are working with, you will be able to naturally exude confidence. And confidence sells.

Your Avatar does not have to be a person or group for whom you have the highest passion. Instead, choose an Avatar who is someone that you are good at treating; the more good you are, the better. In my opinion, it is best to choose an Avatar who is someone that is in your "wheelhouse" for working with versus choosing an Avatar for whom you have a lot of passion - unless, of course, you happen to be damn good at working with individuals who happen to be in your passion.

But why not choose your passion? A few factors go into this. You may be super-passionate about a group of people who simply do not have financial resources. I am not suggesting that these individuals should not receive care. They absolutely deserve to have access to your gift. But as a business owner trying to create time freedom for yourself and your family, you may have to serve others – first. In other words, build your Legacy so that you can have the resources to work with those for whom you have immense passion.

In my opinion, I believe that is also important to do a gut-check on the motivation behind your passion. Why do you desire to work with said individuals? For example, you may wish to work with golfers or high-end executives, because they tend to have expendable income. But if that is your only reason for choosing this population, then you may lack the emotional connection with these groups that will lead to worthwhile success. Additionally, if THEIR money is what drives you, then potentially many important steps may be overlooked. You have to know your people; understand them; know their fears, their values, what is truly important to them. It is so important to be able to separate the potential money earned from making the sell. When the focus is on serving the person in THEIR best interest, more sales will happen. Yes, as an entrepreneur you are looking to make money. But, when an Avatar is chosen because of the potential money, first and foremost, then struggles may be ahead.

When I work with my coaching students, I have them answer a Foundational Questionnaire in the beginning. A vast majority of the FQ focuses on that student's Avatar.   These questions include:

1. What are you passionate about?
2. Whom are you willing to treat for free?
3. Describe your Avatar in detail:
     Age, Sex, Family, Hobbies, Job, etc.
4. What are your Avatar's fears?
5. What are your Avatar's Limiting Beliefs?
6. The consequences of your Avatar "failing"?
7. What will your Avatar gain by "winning"?

When a student begins the program, the student is first challenged with answering these questions before Avatar is even discussed. It is important for the entrepreneur to go through this routine, themselves, for a couple of reasons. First, I have already outlined that if you ain't first, your last. Secondly, when the person has answered these questions, he or she will be much more skilled at taking the potential customer through the process of Lead to Buyer.

These questions are designed to challenge the budding entrepreneur to reflect and to gain a true understanding of whom the target audience will be. Knowing all the possible ins and outs of your Avatar plays a huge roll in a number of elements that will determine the fate of your success. Understanding what makes your intended customer "tick" will help you to create an effective message to that person; one that garners their attention and persuades them to want to hear more about what you have to say. When you have identified what the person stands to "lose" by not making the transformation that they desire, you increase the likelihood that they are going to take a step forward with you. Showing them what THEY are going to achieve by "winning" will them to walk right across the "Epiphany Bridge" and purchase from you.

Let me share an example, if I may. Do you mind? Ok. Fantawesome.

If your Avatar happens to be working with high school athletes, specifically elite swimmers, there are questions for you to get to, and things for you to understand as the seller (i.e. provider) to help a potential customer cross that bridge. Let's say that Michael (no, not Phelps) has been complaining of shoulder pain that is affecting his swimming. Michael and his parents are approached with the typical "he needs physical therapy to correct the shoulder and to resolve the pain." They ask how much will this cost, and you tell them $175. They may buy, but the chances are going to be fairly low. The reason is because you have provided a solution to only the superficial problem, which is the shoulder pain. In order to build trust and to help them cross the bridge over to buying, you have to be able to hold their hands and walk them across.

49

What does that look like? It involves asking questions that get to the real heart of the matter. I hate to say it, but the typical provider will ask about pain, and then say: "I can fix it." But the pain may not be the real issue. Therefore, you have to dive into discovering what are the real internal struggles. Further questioning reveals that Michael has a huge upcoming swim meet that has implications for attending Nationals. More questions lead you to discovering that last year Michael qualified for Nationals and just missed out on Junior Olympic team qualifying by a mere fraction of a second. This year is his year. Michael has gained quite the reputation. He is looked up to by his peers, and respected by his rivals. What does his shoulder pain potentially represent?

If Michael doesn't perform as expected in the upcoming meet, he doesn't qualify for Nationals where he is expected to take at least a silver medal. Failing to take top three at Nationals means that his shot at the Junior Olympic swim team is over. Making the regular Olympic swim team will become a near impossibility. Michael may fear that not making it to the Junior Olympic team will mean that his status amongst his friends and rivals will decline; especially if he doesn't even qualify for Nationals. Michael has put in countless hours of early morning practice. His parents have spent nearly above their means to give Michael this opportunity.

Now can you see what is really at stake here for Michael? It isn't his shoulder pain. His shoulder pain is simply the conversation starter from his standpoint. When you can become a private investigator, not in the cause of pain, but in determining the real internal struggles that someone is facing, then you will be able to walk that person across the bridge. You will convert a lead into a customer.

Tip:

People do not seek help because of pain. People seek out help because pain is preventing them from what they love to do. It is your job as the entrepreneur offering solutions to figure out what the person stands to lose by not doing what they love to do. Likewise, what do they stand to gain by achieving success through what you provide.

However, persuading someone to buy involves more than knowing their fears and what they want to achieve. It is equally important to have a handle on what their Limiting Beliefs are – or, what they may be. Why? Because you will have every objection in the book thrown at you as to why the person is unsure of buying from you: cost, got to check with the spouse, just not sure, and many more. In order to sell, you have to be good at persuading. To be good at persuading, you must be confident. And to be confident, you must be prepared. When you can anticipate the objections to buying, you will know exactly how to respond. Doing so with confidence will help to change the person's limiting beliefs and persuade them to buy.

I know what you are probably saying in your head right now: "But I want to treat everyone. If I niche down, aren't I going to limit myself? I am not going to get as many clients. People who I can help will think I can't help them, or won't help them."

There is a basic rule in business, any business, which says that if you are trying to speak to everyone, you are speaking to no one. Speaking to everyone leaves the potential customer unsure of if you are actually addressing THEIR needs, wants, and desires. To speak to everyone means that you are using broad stroke terms that do not provide clarity. People want clarity when buying. Remember: people want to be the hero of a story. When a sales pitch is put out there that says: "Hey! I help everybody!" then that potential customer feels like another face in the crowd. They don't feel special. And it leaves them thinking: "Yeah, I hear ya. But that isn't really me right now."

It may seem hard to fathom, but niching down will allow you to scale up. Having a clearly defined message targeting a specific person will actually attract the attention of others. Here are a couple of examples...

I recently saw an ad for Coppertone sunblock. The tv ad showed a guy and a gal skateboarding and riding in-line skates. The voice over told me: "Coppertone sunblock is great for the skateboarder and in-line skaters who are spending the day turning tricks." (or something to that effect). The entire commercial showed only these two individuals and no one else. I know that Coppertone has been around for quite some time, but do you think it's reasonable to think that someone else was watching that commercial and thinking: "You know, that might protect me from the sun while I play golf, go to the beach, sit out at my daughter's soccer games, and on and on and on."

Here is another example of a message having an effect by being directed at a specific person. Let's say that you and I are sitting in the back row of a lecture. There is some chattering going on in the room, including you and me. The presenter politely asks that (we) keep the chatter down so that others can hear. Now, you and I sitting in the back row look at each other and kind of say "oops" and shrug it off; thinking: "Well, she isn't really talking to us. Besides, we are in the back row, anyway." And the chattering continues. You KNOW you have been in plenty of those situations. Right?

Now the presenter stops and says: "Hey. (Jeremy) and David in the back row, simmer down, please. You are disturbing others from being able to hear the presentation. WHOA. She just spoke directly to US. We had better comply with what she just requested. And, guess what?? Everybody else in the room just turned to look at who (Jeremy and David) are, and they also heard the message LOUD and CLEAR.

Make sense? Clear as mud?

Niche down until it hurts, and you will gain a lot more clients than telling EVERYONE: "I do this, and this, and this, and this, and this. I can help you, and you, and you, and you, and you."

Trust me.

Take Home Points

- What are YOU Passionate about?
- Who would you work with for free?
- Niche down until it hurts for optimization.
- Learn everything about your Avatar.
- Knowing your Avatar helps with messaging.
- Clarity in your message will attract others.
- People do not seek help because of pain. They seek help because the pain is preventing them from what they love.
- Not being able to do what they love poses Internal Struggles. It is your job to figure those out in order to help them cross the Epiphany Bridge and buy

8
WHERE DO YOU WANT TO BE?

"Where do you want to be in six months, a year from now, in five years, in 10 years?" If you have dreaded answering this question, then raise your hand. I DESPISED answering this, regardless of the reason. I even disliked coming up with goals to write down on patient evaluations. I always felt as though I was concocting something in order to appease a third-party payer. Was it not good enough to get the person back to where THEY wanted to be? Shouldn't that be the only goal that mattered?

I am not sure why I always hated writing down goals. Perhaps because doing so made me think. They made me project forward. OMG, if I write something down, then that means I might have to actually try to live up to it! In other words, setting goals give you direction and hold you accountable. People thirst for direction, and they want to be held accountable. But, at the same time, being held accountable is something that often makes people a bit nervous. People tend to avoid situations in which there are expectations because the process involves getting uncomfortable with being outside the status quo. Wolfe's Law states that bone grows in response to stress. Just as in Wolfe's Law, we cannot grow in our business unless we endure things that stress us. In order to be a successful entrepreneur, it is a pretty darn good idea to know where you are headed and what you need to do to get there. Having a system in place to keep you on track is important otherwise, you will find yourself kicking cans – aka procrastinating - and getting nowhere.

Goals need to be established and written down for a host of reasons. As I mentioned, goals hold you accountable. This is perhaps the greatest push to give oneself. Otherwise, you will be kicking those cans for far too long. When there is something to hold you accountable, the motivation to get things done increases considerably. Can I be honest here? A lot of people talk. Many don't act. We need those motivators to knock us upside the head in order to keep taking steps.

The clarity that goals provide is essential for knowing where you are headed. With clarity comes focus, and being focused allows one to achieve one's greatest potential. One of the biggest reasons that many people fail to achieve their potential – whether it be professionally, or athletically – is that they do not write down where they hope to be one day. How do goals assist in achieving full potential? Short-term goals serve as markers that can be checked. This provides a visual to one's progress. Checking off goals makes it easy and fun to look back on the journey. Documenting the progress is another way to maintain the motivation to keep moving forward.

One beautiful thing about going on a journey is that the path to the destination occasionally has roadblocks. Goals, particularly larger goals, are rarely conquered by way of a direct path, certainly not an easy path. Creativity is often required to navigate through the ride. In this process, one learns new ways to solve challenges. Being able to problem solve will become a necessary skill as you embark on entrepreneurialism.

Along the way, one will discover one's own strengths and weaknesses. I was once asked how this was so. If you are accomplishing goals that involve simply getting sh## done, then chances are that you are strong in organization. Suppose that in starting out on your journey you have the goal of walking into 10 businesses that could be potential referral sources – doctor offices, gyms, specialty athletic stores, home care giving offices, etc. Let's say that when you leave each location you feel as though you completely stumbled over your words, and that you did a pretty bad job of conveying your message. Then I would say that you just learned that one of your weaknesses is communication. As I discussed way back in an earlier chapter, Communication is the single greatest skill to develop in order to find success in whatever you do.

If you can relate to the scenario that I just described, do not let this increase your anxiety about moving forward. Notice that I said: "Communication is the single greatest skill TO DEVELOP in order to find success." There are myriads of people out there that are highly successful in their business that could sell ice to an Eskimo, and they would tell you that starting out they couldn't sell a glass of water to a wanderer in the desert. How do you get better at communicating, and, thus, selling? You have to put in the reps. Repetitions. Keep taking steps. Keep doing the thing. Keep screwing up. Eventually, you will realize that your approach needs to change. It may be in what you say, or how you say it. But something needs to change. Sometimes, it is merely the fact that you need to say something a thousand times before you get comfortable saying it. What I just described here was a combination of what Goals do for you. They help you to identify weaknesses (and strengths) – in this case, that you stink at communicating your message. They help you to alter your approach, become adaptive, learn to make pivots – here, you figured out what to say and how to say it. They teach you to be resilient. In learning how to better communicate, you didn't give up. And, Goals allow you to document your progress and to serve as motivators. It would be very easy to reflect back on that first day when you completely bombed in front of 10 different people. Knowing that you figured out how to better talk to people gives you a newly found confidence, and THAT is motivation to keep moving forward.

It setting goals it is important to have a blend of various types of goals. Meaning, have short term and long-term goals. Have goals that you know that you can easily conquer, because you will need to taste accomplishment along the way. This will help you to stay motivated. Have goals that stretch you a bit – make you a little uncomfortable. Being uncomfortable is where you will find your most growth. Finally, you should write down one or two goals that completely scare the crap out of you. Why? Because in attempting to get there, you will take yourself pretty darn far.

Your "end goal" should not be something safe, something that you feel pretty certain that you will reach. Safe goals lead to complacency, and they prevent you from finding the greatness that you are destined to achieve.

Take Home Points

Goals –
- Give CLARITY
- Hold you ACCOUNTABLE
- Keep you FOCUSED
- Provide MARKERS to see PROGRESS
- Offer MOTIVATION
- Help to achieve POTENTIAL
- Develop PROBLEM SOLVING skills
- Identify STRENGTHS and WEAKNESSES
- Help you to become RESILIENT

9

INVITE THE PAPARAZZI

Let's take a moment to think about the various businesses that you know, both globally and in your hometown. Chances are you immediately thought of companies like Nike, Adidas, Apple, Microsoft, Chase, Wells-Fargo, Target, Home Depot, Lowe's, ACE Hardware, along with a gazillion other businesses. What about locally? What businesses can you think of that are local to your area? I am certain that there are a few law firms that tap on your shoulder every other commercial. How about physician's groups, hospitals? Are there any well-known therapy clinics?

Now flip it and think about those stores that you have been too that had amazing goods and products, but there seemed to hardly ever be anyone in the store. You may be fascinated by the specialty items they have, or the uniqueness of the products they sell. As you wander around the shop you ponder at how do they even stay in business, because no one is in the store. Chances are that you have been to a little hole-in-the-wall, family run restaurant that served food that was out of this world, or it was pretty darn good, at least. Each time you visit you say to yourself: "I can't believe that no one is here. This place is so good." You keep going back on occasion because it is your best-kept secret in the world.

We all know those "best kept secrets". But, let me tell you, being a best-kept secret is not what you want your business to be known for. Back in Chapter 2 (The Four Corners) I spoke briefly about the need of having a Presence. Having a presence is not just about location. In fact, location is the least of your worries – in my opinion. Location certainly helps, but more importantly, do people even know about you? There are two primary reasons why any business fails, aside from a restaurant having consistently crappy service, and even crappier food: 1) you simply decide to quite; 2) no one knows that you exist. Location won't really matter all that much as long as you do one thing: become Famous. I have a reality check for you. The famous line from the movie, Field of Dreams, "Build it and they will come", is not going to get you famous. Just because you have established yourself as a business, and some local, insignificant publication reported it for a week does not mean that the phone is going to start ringing off the hook. That happens only in the movie. You are going to have to take action beyond establishing your LLC in order to become famous.

Since you are reading this book, chances are that you may be building your mobile business of some sort. Therefore, your location is everywhere, for the most part. Still, people must know that you exist in the world in order for them to call you. If you are developing a brick-and-mortar location it is still more advantageous for you to become famous rather than picking the perfect location; although, again, location never hurts. Honestly, I have seen hundreds of stores with great locations shut down. I have also seen great stores and restaurants with "tough" locations have to close their doors. The success with location has multiple variables. Since this book is about the Mobile Entrepreneur, let's focus on becoming Famous.

What does that mean, exactly, to become famous? Simply, make yourself become known in the community. How do you do that? You pound the pavement. You knock on doors. You ask to speak in front of groups. You host workshops and talks. You write blogs. You follow people on Facebook, Instagram, LinkedIn, or wherever else your audience might be. People need to know that you are out there. You must build your audience. The phone is not going to ring because you acquired your LLC and developed a website.

There is a very important reason to work on your famousity: it establishes you as an Authority and the Go-To person for what you do. Trust me, I talk to a lot of people who feel that they are not really an authority on what they do. The truth is, you just need to know a little bit more than the person who is asking you for help. AND, making yourself famous helps to elevate your status in other people's minds. Let me share a quick story to help illustrate how putting one's self out there really does work.

My wife and I started broadcasting a Facebook LIVE show on Sunday's called "The Wine Down". I got the idea to do this purely for the enjoyment of doing something with my wife. I was accustomed to doing Facebook LIVES. However, my wife did not even like posting pictures that included her in them. This was going to be interesting! Anyway, I apologize for the ADD moment there. Each week I tell the audience very early in the introduction: "We are not trained sommeliers, or wine snob-a-seurs. We are just Cara and David bringing to you our Southern Charm as we review a nice bottle of wine." We do carry out a little research for the show, sharing some legit information on the grape, the winery, and a bit of history about the location. Our credentials? We like to drink wine; my wife more so than me. We tend to drink Pinot Noir, Garnacha, and Red Blends the most. The greatest attractor for us in buying a bottle happens to be what the label looks like. (Believe it or not, studies have shown that people DO tend to buy a wine because of the label.) We have been doing the show since August of 2018. To this day, I still cannot pick up on all the flavor and aromas of oak, elderberry, tobacco, cherry, honey, charcoal, rose, sardines, garlic, and everything else that these wines supposedly possess. To me, the wine tastes like wine. Although, I must say, I am getting better and detecting the finish. And I certainly know when I like the wine, or not. Anyhow, you kind of get the idea, right? My wife and I open a bottle of wine on Sundays, and we drink it for the world to see. And you know what happens on a fairly regular basis? We get people reaching out to us in one way or another asking for our opinions and recommendations on a wine, because we are "the experts." Why are we the experts? We consistently show up in front of people sharing some information about wine.

Becoming famous has importance beyond people knowing who you are. Do you know why these reverse mortgage companies, weight-loss companies, cosmetic companies, and every business and product company out there that is playing on the big stage casts a famous person in their ads? Right, because you know the person. But that is not the only reason. Tom Selleck tells me every day to think about buying a reverse mortgage. Why does the company have Tom Selleck trying to persuade me to buy? Because Tom is so well known that he is a person that one can trust. Becoming famous also means that you are developing the trust of others in you. In order for your audience to listen to you, and to want to buy from you, they must first trust you. Your audience finds you, talks about you, trust you, by you becoming famous. So, embrace the bright lights.

Take Home Points

- Failure comes from simply quitting, or no one knowing that you exist
- In order to succeed, you must become Famous
- Becoming Famous leads to building Trust
- Becoming Famous sets you up as an Authority
- Build your "Famousity" by consistently showing up

10
IT'S SHOWBIZ, BABY

In the previous chapter, I discussed becoming famous. So much of success is dependent upon people knowing that you are out there with a solution to their problem. With fame comes recognition and trust. The public must first trust you before they will buy from you. I think it is important to take "famousity" to a higher level. In order to maximize your potential, you need to become an Entertainer.

Buying and selling is merely a transfer of energy. People naturally feed off of it. Truth be told, people crave it. Decisions are made from energy. Why do you think clothing stores have hip music pumping in the dressing rooms? That's right! When you are trying on those tight pants and the lighting is good, the mirror is in your favor, and the music has you bouncing your head, your thought is "Damn, I make these pants look gooood." All that energy is being transferred. And, guess what? You buy those pants.

Being an entertainer is a very effective way to transfer energy. However, I know what you may be thinking right now: "But, I'm not an entertainer." I coach a lot of therapists, and this is something I often hear in one shape, form, or fashion. Let me give you a real example of a conversation that I frequently have. My mentor and coach, Greg Todd, is well known for wearing tight, muscle bound super hero t-shirts. If you have watched any of his Facebook LIVES, you also know that to say that he gets a little hyped during his LIVE is a wee bit of an understatement. During his LIVES within his coaching platforms he infuses music. Watching and listening is a straight up party. Music or not, "GT" brings so much energy that the viewer is pumped. When GT makes an offer to buy, he gets roughly a 15% conversion rate, according to the man, himself. A 15% conversion may sound low. But in business, that is not too shabby, I tell you. Create positive energy and people will buy.

I talk to many people who have apprehensions about doing Facebook LIVES. Having their image appear on social media leaves them looking like a deer in the headlights. Those who follow Greg Todd often say: "I am not hype like GT." I tell them: "That's ok. You don't have to be; just be YOU." Being an entertainer does not mean that you have to produce hype social media LIVES. You just have to transfer energy – your energy – to your audience. This can be done through a variety of mediums. If you enjoy being in front of the camera, then do Facebook and Instagram LIVES. Perhaps you are more of a low-key person who avoids the limelight, and you are more comfortable with crafting a story. Then writing blogs can be a fantabulous way for you to share your message. Do you have the Gift of Gab, but prefer to stay behind the camera? A podcast just may be right up your alley. At the very minimum, when face to face with your customers and potential customers, be engaging and transfer positive energy.

Denzel Washington, Leonardo DiCaprio, Tom Hanks, Meryl Streep, Viola Davis, Oprah Winfrey are all powerful actors and actresses. Will Ferrell, Kevin Hart, Steve Carell, Jamie Foxx, Melissa McCarthy, Amy Schumer, Tina Fey, Leslie Jones, and Whoopi Goldberg all are on the A-List as well. The two groups I mentioned consist of actors and actresses with completely different styles. However, all of them (and scores more) have two things in common: they are all entertainers, and they all move people's emotions. In each one's own unique way, they transfer energy to their audience. This energy not only leaves their audience feeling good about purchasing a ticket, the energy also brings the audience back for the next movie. The success that each actor and actress achieve is driven by each being their authentic self.

There are two reasons why it is important to be authentically you. First, people want consistency. The "you" that the customer sees in whatever type of social media post you run, or presentation that you give, better be the "you" that they experience when face to face. Consistency brings clarity, and people need clarity on what you are presenting.

Secondly, being authentically you helps to attract those whom you best serve. If you are a high-energy person, you are more likely to interact best with like-minded individuals. You may become frustrated with quiet, timid people. Conversely, if you have a low-key personality, then a highly driven customer may lose interest in buying from you. When you are you, you will attract people like you. I can promise you that when you are working with someone who jives with you, your confidence skyrockets. And, you know what comes with confidence? Energy. Buying and selling involves energy transfer. In your own way, become an entertainer. And, as I said previously, enjoy the bright lights!

Take Home Points

- Become an Entertainer
- Be authentically YOU
- Transfer energy to your audience
- Enjoy the Bright Lights

11
SHOW ME THE MONEY

One of the first questions I am asked is: "How much should I charge?" This is a darn good question. Honestly, I don't know the answer! But, I can help you to determine what you should be charging. Several factors and considerations come into play. While the factors and considerations are the same for everyone, the specifics of them are independent from person to person.

First, it is a good idea to do some research to find out what other people in your area are charging. You don't want to be the cheapest in town; nor do you want to be way above everyone else in your pricing. You can always start with a price and increase it. In fact, regardless of where you set your initial price, you WILL increase it over time. A suggestion that I offer is to start with a lower price (one that is in the range that they are contemplating). There is a reason why I like this strategy. People who are first starting out in an entrepreneurial journey, particularly therapists, tend to not be accustomed to, or comfortable with, asking people for money. When the time comes that you have to state your price, the words have to roll off your tongue like melted butter unapologetically. Stating your price has to be said with confidence. I'm going to say it again. Confidence sells. If you hem and haw about your price, then the buyer receives the energy that you are not comfortable with your offer. This also tells the buyer that you do not believe that you are worth the price. For some, saying a lower price may help them to gain the confidence to tell people what they are worth. Taste success first, and then increase your price. Eventually you will start to become irritated that you are charging such a low price. Thus, when you decide to raise your rate you will be confident in doing so, and saying so, because you will have reached a point where you are saying to yourself: "I am worth this!"

A great question to ask yourself is what would you be willing to pay you to provide you with services? If you answer that you wouldn't feel comfortable paying you $150 (for example), then there is no way that you are going to transfer a confident energy to the buyer over your price. Here is another tip: If people are agreeing to your price with no hesitation, then chances are that your price is too low. When entrepreneurs find that they are struggling to get the price they are asking, the first line of defense is typically to lower their price. That fixes everything, right? Wrong. If the price appears to be too high, then you must increase the value of what you have to offer. If customers are expecting a concierge service, but what is being delivered is no different than what a staff employee may provide, then asking premium dollar won't work.

When determining your rate, it is important that you acknowledge that you are now an entrepreneur attempting to generate income on your own. There won't be any paychecks magically appearing in your employee box every two weeks. Not only are you embarking on the entrepreneurial journey, but you are also attempting to build a business. And, no, the two are not one in the same.

One of the most important things for the budding entrepreneur to do is something that I addressed roughly 68 pages ago. You got to have a mind shift in your thinking. In the case of making money, you have to pivot away from the mentality of you just want to help people. That is an answer you gave when applying to school to start your career path. For many of you, being an entrepreneur may not have been in your Johari Window at the time. I guarantee that most of you are now seeking a change because you have discovered or become frustrated that you are in a situation where you feel as though you cannot really help people.

Now, don't get me wrong. You are going to help people. In fact, you can help others more so now than when you were receiving a paycheck. Your two primary Whats for doing your own thing are, undoubtedly, that you are going to work with clients the way that you want to work with them. You also can now spend more time working with your clients in the way that they desire. If you are considering the cash-based model, people ARE WILLING to pay for real value. So, do not feel badly about charging for your services. Unfortunately, schools tend to teach us to feel badly about asking for money from our customers. The common message I heard throughout my physical therapy schooling was: "Work hard, and the money will be there." I heard the same thing during my 19 years of being an employee.

When it comes to people paying for value, it is up to you to figure out what that value is for the client. The fact that you spend a full hour with clients may not necessarily be what they view as a value. If you can resolve an issue faster, that may be what some want. In general, being able to provide hope and the promise of a transformation is what people are willing to buy. The customer wants clarity in communication. They want confidence. They want answers. I will tell you this. The fact that it cost you well over $100k to obtain your degree is NOT what your client holds as value.

In establishing your rates, it is important to keep in mind that you are not generating revenue to simply pay your bills. You are generating an income to create the life that you desire. With this comes the responsibility you have to yourself of planning for the future; including unfortunate possibilities. As an entrepreneur, you are not building up paid time off or sick days. If your rate is just enough to pay your bills, what happens if you catch a nasty crud and you cannot work for two or three days? A very common reason that people decide to be in charge of themselves is that they want to be able to take vacations without asking for permission 30 days in advance. If you are not working, you are not making money. You are likely to also be spending money while you are enjoying your free time. What you now have is a double whammy. If you are merely paying your bills, how are you going to plan for retirement? Your rates should help you to prepare for these things. There is one thing that I have come to understand after years of being employed, and now having my own business: no one ever gets ahead with a paycheck as an implementer. So, get comfortable asking for money.

Now that I have said all of this, the easiest way to determine your price is to reverse engineer it. Start by asking yourself how much money do you want to gross at the end of the year; then work backwards. You also need to have an idea of how many clients per week that you want to see. Here is an example:

Let's say that you want to gross $150K for the year. That averages out to $12,500 each month. You are thinking you want to see no more than 25 visits/week. Since you want to enjoy your weekends (I'm just saying), then that would mean you would see 5 visits each day, Monday through Friday. You need to average $3,125 per week to reach $12,500. $3,125 divided by 25 would mean that your rate should be $125 per visit.

Again, this scenario is merely an example to help walk you through the process of determining your price. But, it is a very real example. Here is what I like about determining your price with reverse engineering. It forces you to define a year-end goal, and you now know what you need to do to reach that goal. Knowing what your end-goal is will help you with your confidence in stating your price. Knowing WHY you are charging $125 for a session makes it much easier to command it. When you are asking for an arbitrary price with no rhyme or reason to it, you are more likely to be apologetic about your rate.

Take Home Points

- Have an understanding as to what others within your profession and outside of it are charging
- Would you pay yourself the rate that you are asking?
- You can always increase your rate
- If people are not flinching at your price, it may be too low

- Don't lower your price. Increase the value of what you have to offer.
- Generating income is now on YOU
- People will pay for real value
- Don't feel badly about charging for your services
- You are generating revenue to do more than to simply pay your bill

12
I AM THE CAPTAIN

Smart Success Physical Therapy is an organization of physical therapist, occupational, therapists, registered dieticians, MD's, chiropractors, massage therapists, nurses, COTA's, PTA's, students, and pre-graduate school students. More than being an organization, it is a family, really. SSPT, founded by my mentor, Greg Todd, has over 500 members at the time of this writing. I found SSPT and joined in late January 2018. Almost immediately I was dubbed the nickname, "Captain". Being named co-rookie of 2018 for all of SSPT was an honor of which I am very proud. Prior to joining SSPT did I ever imagine that colleagues from all across the country would look up to me in such a way as to call me Captain. I suddenly had people reaching out to me on a regular basis asking for advice. I started a private Facebook group, The Mobile PT League (at this time with 2300 members in just over a year and a half). Therapists from The League were turning to me – ME – for advice. Honestly, I was quite dumbfounded by it all. I was (and still am) certainly proud and grateful, but dumbfounded none-the-less. The Mobile PT League, a Facebook community regarding one of the hottest and fastest growing sectors in the therapy realm, continues to see growth. I have a coaching program and co-host a podcast that is downloaded literally worldwide with my business partner, Josh Payne. There is an on-line course available also. I have one that I co-authored with my friend, F Scott Feil. Yet, two years ago from this writing, no therapist aside from those with whom I previously worked knew that I existed. How has all of this happened? I changed the Beliefs that served me. And this is an important question to ask yourself; particularly if you are feeling stuck: Are your Beliefs serving you.

I conduct a lot of coaching and mentoring calls each week. Without a doubt, one of the number one things that I help clinicians work through is to get out of their own way. I spoke about BELIEF early on in this Roadmap Guide, but I want to address it just a bit further, because a person's beliefs are quite often the primary things that are preventing them from taking action. For anyone looking to build their own dreams, it is important to ask yourself: "Are your Beliefs serving you?"

Many of us are told from an early age that there are things that we cannot do, people we cannot become. Others rightfully share their own opinions of things being the way they are because, it is what it is. Thus, we adopt certain beliefs about things. How many of us have heard a gazillion times from our parents and grandparents that "Patience is a virtue", or that "Good things come to those who wait." As a result, we learn to wait patiently for good things to come our way. Subliminally, our brains tell us to NOT take action. Be patient; wait, and good things will come our way. Meanwhile, we see others finding success in their endeavors, leaving us wondering: "When will my day come?" We can easily become envious of the fruits that others are enjoying. The reality is that the difference between those who are winning and you is simply that they took action. They may not have any more skill than you. They may not be any smarter than you. They may not have a better product than you. What they have that you don't is action.

I was on a mentoring call with "Joe", a new grad that was interested in opening his practice. He asked what continuing education courses he should take, because he felt that he needed to gain more knowledge before he could open his practice. Naturally, I questioned "Joe" as to why he needed continuing education prior to hanging his shingle. My eyes rolled at what he told me – not at him, but at the source of his limiting belief. "Joe" had graduated from one of the local physical therapy programs only three months prior. He had already discovered that being an employee seeing 35 patients/day was not his thing. Therefore, he was anxious to build his own empire. I asked "Joe" what was holding him back. He told me that he had run his idea by a couple of his professors, and both told him that they would not come to him as clients because he lacked the knowledge and skill to effectively treat them at this point. Their strong recommendation was that he go through the school's one-year residency program before attempting to open his own doors.

Wait. Say what? This was the reason why my eyes nearly went into spasm as they reached the pinnacle of their circular motions within the sockets. Here was a Doctor of Physical Therapy being told by his professors that, essentially, he did not know enough to make a difference in a person's life. My first response to this ridiculous reasoning was to ask that if he (or anyone else graduating) was not yet ready to help others, then why did the school release him out into the wild? People, I hear these types of stories all the time. And, I'm guessing you have been told the same somewhere along the way – that you are not ready to impact lives without the supervision of a "more experienced" clinician. I have even heard other clinicians speak of new grads in a negative light, because the said new grad was feeling restless and wanted to head West. These veterans felt that one should remain caged for a minimum of 5 years before exploring. Well, I have plenty of examples of clinicians who are out of school anywhere from literally just graduated to less than two years, and they are already crushing it with their own gig.

I asked "Joe" what was his passion. He said that he had years of experience in Ju-Jitsu. He loved the sport. In fact, he had been treating a few people from his gym recently. Hmmm. I gave "Joe" a scenario. I asked that if he were to treat someone from the gym with low back pain, for example, what would his program look like? He told me that he had just completed a care plan with a guy that fit this example. "Joe" proceeded to outline his program with the client, a program that impressed the heck out of me! Here was a new grad taking someone through a SOLID treatment plan. He had addressed everything beautifully. My feedback to him was just that.
Then "Joe" became a little more upbeat. He said this to me: "The cool thing is that the guy called me to say that he is back to fully

training with no pain or fear, and he is now ready to compete at the World Championships next month."

O.K. Stop.

Joe, did you hear what you just told me? You took a world-class athlete who was injured; you rehabbed him, and now he is ready to compete at the World Championships with full confidence in his abilities. I asked: "Do you think you know enough to make a difference in someone's life? Do you really think that it is necessary to go through a year residency before you start along your yellow brick road?" I think you can guess what "Joe's" answer was. The cool thing was this. "Joe" said that as he was describing his program with this athlete that in his head he was thinking what a pretty rock star approach it had been.
Here was a clinician fully ready to conquer the world, yet his beliefs were not serving him. Had I not asked the two simple questions of: 1) what is holding you back; and 2) describe a treatment plan, "Joe" would very easily be putting his dream on hold for another two years, minimum, because his belief was that he was not yet smart enough.

Too often our beliefs are forced upon us like the example of "Joe". But sometimes our beliefs are shaped by a prior experience. Perhaps presenting in front of the class would give you a terrible case of the stomach knots. The "pre-game" jitters would make you shiver as if the air conditioning was set at 40 degrees. Yet, you somehow managed to be sweating profusely. Your mouth felt as dry as if you had eaten a full sleeve of saltine crackers, and not a drop of liquid in sight. Your heart rate matched that of a hummingbird. To finish things off, you would become completely out of breath from speaking so frantically. If this describes your speaking experiences, then it would be very easy to tell yourself that you do not do well speaking in front of others. This would lead to you telling yourself that you stink at any kind of marketing.

Maybe a task given to you in the clinic was to convince your patients to join the "post rehab" program being offered. Despite your persistent efforts, none of your clients ever signed up. Chances are that you begin to tell yourself that you are the worst salesperson ever.

Some limiting beliefs can be a combination of taught experience and from what others tell us. The most perfect example is something that I guarantee that you are struggling with right now, and what was discussed in the previous chapter: setting your rate – that is, if you are thinking of the cash-based route.

We are not taught in schools to ask clients for money. Insurance is typically the only thing that is discussed. Therefore, even someone like myself who started my cash practice after 19 years, we have never asked for money. When the typical co-pay ranges from $20-$100, we have a belief that no one would be willing to pay more than their co-pay. Additionally, we are told by our colleagues, and others, that people will not pay for physical/occupational therapy. I certainly heard that multiple times as I was about to dive head first into the water. When sharing with others my plan, it was repeatedly suggested to me that I had better take insurance, because people will not pay. I heard this from family, former spouse (who is a PT), other therapists, my pool guy, and so on. But, I stuck to my plan because I had already been introduced to a population of people who were willing to pay for quality. The result? I see far fewer clients than when I worked in the clinic, and I have doubled my salary. That's right. People won't pay.

Take my history, for example. It took me three years of applying to schools before finally being accepted. Despite doing well in physical therapy school, I failed my comprehensive oral exam that was required prior to going out on full time clinical rotations. Later, I passed the national licensure exam by one point. Undoubtedly, I have long battled the limiting belief that I am not smart enough. Quite often this belief caused me to lack confidence with particular clients. I would even with hold from participating in conversations with friends or colleagues for fear of appearing stupid.

Starting this book was delayed due to one of my limiting beliefs. For years I have struggled with feeling as if my mind was a complete blank whenever I would be out with others and an engaging conversation amongst everyone was taking place. I would sit quietly, listening to everyone; occasionally nodding my head and smiling. What I did not do was to contribute to the conversation. Why? I literally could not think of a single thing to say, or a single question to ask. Outwardly, I was smiling. However, deep inside I was frustrated and screaming, because I was a total blank. Now, not only was I frustrated that I had nothing to say, but I also feared that I was appearing to be dumb, boring, uninteresting. I have struggled with this for years. Quite frankly, I was scared to write this book because I BELIEVED that I had nothing to say beyond seven or eight pages. My good friend, Jeremy Sutton, was a Blessing on encouraging me to write this.

How can you start to reverse your limiting beliefs? The same way I have worked on mine. I simply started taking steps. I consciously made decisions to DO. I gave myself permission to not know everything. And, something that I spoke about earlier in this book, I began to own my Gift.

But the most valuable thing that I have done is to surround myself with people who have encouraged me in my dreams. I invested in coaching to push me, to hold me accountable, and to teach me how to do things that I either did not know how to do, or I thought I could not do. When you find your tribe of people who are supportive of you, who encourage you, and who lift you up, amazing things start to happen. You begin to believe that you can fly. Better yet, you just might become the damn Captain.

Take Home Points

- Are your Beliefs serving you?
- Things we are told hold us back.
- Our own past experiences hold us back.
- Overcome by taking action.
- Finding your tribe can help you to achieve
- A coach/mentor can help you to get out of your way.

13
DO YOU

Everyone sets out on the entrepreneurial journey with wide eyes, big dreams, visions of bright lights, and money, lots of money. Being an entrepreneur means living life on your terms without having to report to anyone else. Even just saying the word entrepreneur is like saying "la-ti-dah" in a fancy way. However, the entrepreneurial life can spawn seeds of doubt. It is very easy to get caught up in looking to your left and to your right to see what others are doing. Social media provides constant postings of other people winning at the game. Panic ensues. Comparison is the thievery of all dreams.

I was four months into my mobile practice when I heard of some news regarding a fellow co-worker from my previous place of employment had started his own mobile practice (which I already knew, because I had inspired him to do so). My colleague was only a month into his practice, and he was already bringing on another therapist. I was still in the "developing" phase – i.e. trying to grow enough that bills were being paid. Naturally, I freaked out. I literally went into panic mode. Then I noticed that other therapists I knew, who had single therapist clinics, were offering this program and that program. I literally became paralyzed from hyperventilating. I did not know which way to turn, or what my next step should be. I could not even take a step because I was too overwhelmed. My head was spinning and my mind was running like a head with no chicken on it. Or, whatever that saying is. I needed to offer this package to golfers. I needed to provide this information to runners. I needed to speak to these retirement communities about the importance of remaining active. I could do this to target people suffering from back pain. I needed to produce these videos and those mailings. My website needed to be expanded. I needed, I needed, I needed.

Then, I took a deep breath. What I came to realize were two things. I did not need to try to duplicate everything that others were doing. What I needed to do was to stay in my lane, and do one thing well. I could worry about expanding programs and services later.

Motivational speaker, and Chief Encouragement Officer of COMPETE EVERYDAY, Jake Thompson, explains this so well in a very simple way. He speaks of "doing you" to a sprinter ready to run the race. The starting gun fires, and the sprinter explodes out of the blocks. The runner is focused on one thing at that point: getting a strong start. They drive the legs, pump the arms, and come into their posture. They think about keeping the feet under the knees for faster turnover. And then….they begin to wonder what the other racers are doing. They look to their left. They look to their right. They may even try to glance behind them to see who is on the pursuit. These distractions cause the runner to slow down, because the body cannot perform as efficiently when motions are being altered. It's just like when you are driving your car down the road, and you decide to have a little fun by giving the steering wheel little cuts to the left and right – as if you were going through a slalom course. You naturally slow down a bit. This is what happens to the sprinter. The sprinter becomes focused on what is happening elsewhere on the track, and the goal of winning the race is lost.

I also accepted that not everyone's success looks the same, nor does success come at the same time across the board. I had a talk with myself while driving down the road one day. I said: "David, just because one person is seeing 40 visits/week and you are seeing 25 visits, that does not make you unsuccessful. Just because another person offers this program to these particular athletes, that does not mean that you have to offer that, as well." And you know what happened? A boatload of stress was taken off of my shoulders. I could actually stand taller because of it. My breathing returned to normal. I returned to focusing on MY business, not others. Then, my business started to flourish.

When things are not going as you envisioned them, particularly as you are starting out, it is very easy to go into panic mode. You start looking around and paying more attention to what others are doing rather than putting that energy into your own business. The energy that you do give to your business ends up being little darts here and there. In other words, you start trying to speak to everyone; thus, you speak to no one.

This may be a short chapter in this guide, but THIS is exactly why the things I discussed in the beginning are so very important. Having an open mindset vs. closed mindset, a growth mindset vs. fixed helps you to avoid these pitfalls that so easily creep up right in front of you; derailing you from your yellow brick road. Focus on your game plan. Keep taking steps forward. DO YOU.

Take Home Points

- Comparison is the thievery of dreams
- You do not have to be doing what everyone else is doing
- Success looks differently for everyone
- Success comes at different rates
- Stay in your lane

14
BE LIKE MIKE

"Some people want it to happen, some wish it to happen, others make it happen."

Michael Jordan is considered the greatest basketball player to ever grace 94'x50' of hardwood. Much of the younger generation may feel that, perhaps, LeBron James is now the greatest. However, LeBron has often struggled late in big games. As good as Jordan was, he always seemed to thrive the most when everything was on the line. Those who had the pleasure of observing Jordan in practice have said that he often played harder in the practices than he did in the games. Jordan consistently strived to make himself better. But he did something even more important than improving himself. He made those around him better players.

During his hay day, there was a huge marketing campaign that encouraged people to "Be Like Mike." The message was not to challenge young ball players to score 50 points in their next game, or to stick out their tongue as they shoot the ball. The message was about everything that His Greatness embodied.

Michael Jordan represented success from failure.   It has been well publicized repeatedly how "Michael" had been cut from the junior varsity team in high school because he lacked the talent. He responded to that setback by becoming one of the top collegiate recruits in the country just three years later. He epitomized relentlessness and hard work. He was never afraid to take the big shot. The man flat out exuded confidence. What do we know about confidence, not only in sports, but also in business and in life? Confidence wins. Confidence sells.

"I can accept failure, everyone fails at something. But I can't accept not trying."

The keys to success come down to the Three C's: Communication, Confidence, and Consistency. The interesting thing about the Three C's is that each one has an impact on the other two; much like a snowball effect. Earlier in the book I talked about developing a clear and concise message to attract your Roger Federer. A strong message portrays confidence in what you do. Being consistent with your message improves how you communicate, and nurtures your confidence. Consistency in being present (i.e. becoming "famous") builds the confidence that others – like potential customers – have in you. When you are confident in what you have to share with others, your communication skills improve immensely.

You know what's unfortunate? The Three C's are not taught at any point in the educational process. Yes, we are required to give presentations in school. But the manner in which we entertain is not discussed in the feedback. We may receive a lower grade for not showing confidence in our talk. But that is typically where the feedback stops. When I failed my oral comprehensive exams, the faculty's reasoning for their decision was that I did not answer with confidence. The failing grade had nothing to do with whether or not my answers where right or wrong, but that I did not present with confidence. That was fair, and I appreciated that reason. However, ZERO suggestions were given as to how I could improve on my performance for Round 2.

Here is what I want you, the reader, to take from this example. A LOT of people have to work on confidence when it comes to getting across a message. Secondly, if you do not speak with confidence, your audience is not going to have confidence in you.

Aside from the obvious, I bring up confidence for a very important reason. When you are with your client, it is imperative that YOU be the decision maker throughout the process. Your client has chosen YOU to take them through their transformation. They want you to tell them what the game plan looks like. They want you to tell them how often they should see you. And they want to know how long is this going to take. It is your responsibility to be the decision maker. Trust me, it is what they want. Here is helpful tip #5: I have had clients share with me that they were frustrated in their physician visit because the physician did not lead in the decision-making process. Instead, the physician left the option up to the client of how to proceed on a simple step.

When a client asks how many visits, give them a confident answer, even if you are wrong. Your response may sound something like this:

"In my experience, this usual takes on
average about 8 visits (for example).
The number of visits will vary based on
each individual case. I have seen this
resolve in 5 visits, but I have seen this take up to 12 sessions.
When we get to session 5,
I will have a good sense of your progress."

This does a number of things. First, you have answered confidently. You have established an expectation for how long the process will take. However, you have also pre-set the possibility that they may need less or more visits. Therefore, you avoid throwing a surprise at the client late in the game. Here is something that is very important for you to grasp: It is far better to be wrong with confidence than to be right with uncertainty.

I've got another little secret for you. When someone calls to inquire about your services, they are already telling you that they are looking to go through a transformation. They just want to know if you have the solution they are seeking. Therefore, it is your job to not mess it up.

I watched an episode of "Million Dollar Listing" on the BRAVO channel one night. The episode spoke beautifully to being confident, and being the decision maker with your lead/client. A new agent met with potential clients – husband and wife – about listing their New York City apartment. The couple expressed that they were not sure if they were ready to list their property. The new agent told them that he understood and that he didn't want to pressure them into making a decision that they weren't ready to make. He suggested that they think about it for a couple of days and then let him know.

The couple then met with another agent, Ryan Serhant. Ryan is a freakin' Rock Star of an agent. The dude has sold over $1 BILLION in properties. When Ryan met with the couple, they gave him the same story: not sure they were ready to list. They also said that this property was their masterpiece that they had created; therefore, they were not sure they were ready to part with the property. Ryan came back with brilliance. This is what he said: "Look, I know you are wanting to sell. Otherwise, why did you call me? And, yes, this IS a masterpiece that you have created. It's beautiful. But did Picasso stop after he created his first masterpiece? No? He moved on to his next masterpiece, and then the next one. You now have the opportunity to create your next masterpiece."

I'll give you three guesses which agent the couple chose, and the first two guesses don't count.

The first agent failed to identify the couple's inner struggle and biggest fear: could they create another masterpiece. He then backed away from being a decision maker for them. Selling was what they were wanting and ready to do. Serhant pointed that out to them! Thirdly, the agent left the ball in their court by telling them to "Let me know." Many may say that he was being respectful, and not pushy. But, believe me, there is a big difference between being pushy and helping someone to see the decision that they are already wanting to make – and to do so with confidence.

Serhant acknowledged that the couple was already willing to sell; that is why they called him. He then addressed the matter by speaking to their inner-most fear: doubt about creating another masterpiece. Not only did he tell them that they could do it, but he also gave them permission to do so. Boom. Game over. And as Paul Harvey would say: "And now you know the rest of the story."

My apologies for my self diagnosed ADD kicking in. Let's get back to Michael Jordan. When I think about the popular slogan "Be Like Mike", I realize that he so many key points that are discussed in this book. It is a good thing that this wasn't Chapter 1. You would have stopped reading right there!

When it comes to confidence, Jordan possessed it. He WANTED the ball late in the game; especially if a championship was on the line. Far more often than not, he delivered. He played hard night in and night out. There were even some big playoff games where he scored more than 50 points despite reportedly battling flu-like symptoms. He played even harder in practice. He was consistent with his effort. It was his consistency that took him from being cut from the team to being the Greatest of All Time. His actions communicated to the rest of the team "there is no 'I' in me, but there is in 'WIN'".

When I spoke about the importance of goals, I said that one thing that goals allowed us to do was to identify our weaknesses. Jordan had one goal: to win Championships. His pursuit of them was relentless. In fact, he was so relentless that he won three straight, retired, then later returned to the Chicago Bulls to win another three straight Championships. It would be understandable for one to ask that of all of the amazing accomplishments of the man they called "Heir Jordan", in reference to his Nike shoe line "Air Jordan", what weakness could he possibly have – as it related to basketball? The attributes that made Jordan, Jordan were the things that prevented him from ever pursuing coaching. He knew that no single player, let alone an entire team, would ever be as tenacious as he was in practice. He saw too many players "take nights off" during the season. He knew that while every player dreams of winning a title, very few commit themselves to the work that it takes to cradle the trophy with tears of joy. His goal of winning showed him that his weakness was that he had no tolerance for coaching those who were not equally as committed.

Can I digress for another moment? Super. It is not uncommon to see famous athletes around town when living in the Phoenix/Scottsdale area. I have seen countless in all my years of residing her. I literally have had to step aside to avoid walking into the likes of Steve Nash, and Grant Hill. I developed a decent neck strain as I looked up at Shaquille O'Neal as he brushed past me in a bar one night. I chuckled when the great Pittsburg Steeler running back, Franco Harris, introduced himself to me in this manner (and I quote): "Hi. I'm Franco. Please, help me eat these chicken tenders." I thought "Holy Crap! This is Andre Agassi" as I shook his hand in the trainer's room at the local pro tennis event that used to be held in Scottsdale. But no one, NO ONE, ever made me stop dead in my tracks speechless as Michael Jordan did the night I saw him walking out of a restaurant that I was about to enter. There truly was this air about him as he walked by – no pun intended.

In the chapter, "YOU Must Become Your First Customer", I talked about the importance of Delighting yourself and your audience. Jordan famously said: "Just play. Have fun. Enjoy the game." When it comes to being consistent and developing confidence, I love this that His Greatness once shared: "I have failed over and over and over again in my life, and that is why I succeed."

Be like Mike.

Take Home Points

- Three C's to success: Communication, Confidence, Consistency.
- Your client wants you to be the decision maker, so make the decision.
- It is better to be wrong with confidence than to be right with uncertainty.
- Be like Mike.

15

THE OBJECTIVE: LEAVE WITH NOTHING

I mentioned early in the book that one of the best ways to create your presence and to build your famousity involves pounding the pavement. Again, this includes visiting potential referral sources, setting up workshops, giving talks, and participating at events as a vendor. When you do all of these things, your mission is to begin to nurture a relationship. Your objective is to leave with nothing.

You are thinking: "What? Leave with nothing? What in the heck does that mean?" After all, marketing is how we get clients, right? Clients are needed to pay the bills. Leave with nothing? That's right. Leave with nothing. Bear with me.

You first need to understand something about marketing. Marketing is NOT where you get clients. Marketing is where you nurture – educate - potential leads. The purpose of marketing is to start to develop relationships. People buy when they have a relationship with something or someone. Less than 5% of the population is willing to purchase on the initial whim. Most people tend to buy after they have received free. So, how do you get people's interest? You serve. And serve. And serve. And in between the serving you listen. In order to know what to sell to people, and to know what the people are craving to buy, you have got to listen to them. You may have spent $150K on a doctorate degree, but that does not mean that you know how it is that the potential client is looking to spend their money. You have to listen, and they will tell you what it is they want.

For any engagement that you have with a potential client, or referral source, the mindset should be 100% How can I serve this person today? First and foremost, you MUST be interestED; not interestING. Asking questions of others is the best way to generate interest in you. Here's what I mean. Imagine you are on a first date. You are super excited to have the other person know how fantawesome you are, because, well, you are pretty freaking fantawesome. On the date, you spend the entire time telling the other person all about yourself, because you are hoping to really wow them. You may leave the date feeling pretty good about the things you shared. You, yourself, are impressed by all of your amazingness. But, let's think about the other person. Chances are they couldn't wait for the date to end. They probably leave thinking that you were mighty proud of yourself. The chances of a second date are pretty slim.

Now flip the exchange. Instead of you telling the person how incredible you are and giving them all sorts of reasons why they should be impressed, you ask them questions. And, you listen. You are going to leave feeling proud that you asked inquired into the other's life and interests. You will be pleased with yourself that you listened, remarked, and asked follow up questions of further inquiry. Your date leaves feeling like the proud peacock, because they were made the star. Somebody (you) wanted to learn about them. I promise you that the leaves feeling like it was a pretty spectacular evening, and that you are a really great person. The end result: on to date number two. Again, Rule #1 when doing Business-to-Business marketing: be interestED not interestING.

Here is how this may look when meeting with a physician:

First, do a little research on the physician and the practice so you have an idea of anything in which they may specialize. Here is how I would introduce myself:

I am David Bayliff. I have been practicing physical therapy for over 25 years now here in the Valley. Physical therapy is simply a tool that I use to help bring the playground back into people's lives. What I specialize in is helping golfers to develop on and off course management solutions for back pain. (Or, I tailor my message depending on the type of client that I am aiming to gain from the particular physician.)

I continue by saying:

"The reason I wanted to ask for some of your time today is that I am really hoping to learn from you what has made your practice a success; what you feel has been the special sauce that has drawn patients to you when there are so many options out there."

"My clients ask me on a regular basis about a referral to someone or somewhere; for a variety of services, actually. Quite often, they ask if I know of a physician. As I am sure you could respect, when I give a referral for anything, I feel like that my opinion is on the line. Therefore, when it comes to people's health, I look to develop relationships with like-minded providers; those to whom I can confidently refer my clients. I know that you see (X, Y, and Z) types of patients. But, what type of client really excites you? Who is the right person for me to send to you? Like me, I can appreciate that your schedule stays busy. Therefore, I want to make sure I send the right person your way so as to not waste your time with a bobo referral."

I also like to ask questions such as:
"What are your expectations with therapy?"
"What has been your experience, or, rather, your clients' experiences with going to therapy?"
"What have the options been for them if they do not achieve the results they were anticipating?"

Then I leave with stating that *"I certainly have had the perfect client for them in the past, so I am going to have my radar up."* *"And I look forward to developing a relationship with you."*

Boom. Bob's your Uncle.

These same rules apply when leading a workshop, offering screenings at a location, or being present at an event. However, these settings require additional commitment on your part. During these situations, you must enter with the question of How can I serve these people today in the now? Your mission is to answer their questions and to share information that will have massive value to them. Your objective is to leave with nothing.

Regardless of the type of marketing in which you are engaging, it is muy importante that you enter with the mindset of being perfectly fine having provided unbelievable knowledge, yet leaving without a single hot lead; let alone a scheduled visit. Trust me, go into the event not wanting to gain a client, and you are going to win far more often than if your objective is to gain referrals. Your audience – whether it is an audience of one, or a group of 50 – will see right through you if you are there looking to acquire business. They will leave with a sour taste in their mouths. Go forth with wanting to serve – nothing more, nothing less – and you will gain the trust of your audience. The first thing that someone must have before buying: Trust.

Remember that marketing is NOT about client acquisition. Marketing is about client education in order to nurture potential leads. Your objective is to leave with nothing. Work on becoming famous. Serve the heck out of people. Stay consistent in your efforts, and the leads will come.

Take Home Points

- Become Famous by pounding the pavement.
- The Mission of a marketing event is to nurture a relationship.
- The Objective of a marketing event is to leave with nothing.
- Be interestED, not interestING.
- Serve, Serve, Serve, and you will win.

16
THE DISCOVERY VISIT

I have said earlier in the book that only a small percentage of people are willing to buy on a whim. Most need to think a little longer, and receive a little more before opening up the wallet. This is when the Discovery Visit option can be the secret weapon. I use this as an offer to clients when the potential client has reservations to scheduling. However, from the questions I have asked and the information they have given, I can tell that the person needs just a little bit more exposure before buying. More often than not, the reservation is about pricing. Here is an idea of what the conversation may sound like at that point:

Me:
Mr./Mrs. Last Name, I have a strong feeling that you would really like to meet those goals that are important to you. I would love nothing more than for you to conquer them. I know that I can help you through that process. However, I recognize that finances may be somewhat of a barrier at this point, and I respect that. My schedule tends to be tight. Because of that, the individuals I work with are all highly motivated people who want to live their best life possible and to achieve goals very similar to yours. So, what I would like to offer you is a free one-hour discovery visit to see if we are even a good fit for each other. While I would welcome the opportunity to guide you through your process, it is equally as important that you feel that working with me is right for you. Could we schedule the discovery visit and make a decision then?

Depending on the reasoning behind the person calling me, I may add something like this:

It is quite possible that what you have going on needs only a simple tweak in your current program; in which case, you may not even need to see me afterwards. Perhaps you just need a couple of tricks that you can work on yourself.

I did a heap of things here. I offered free – and who resists turning down free? I acknowledged that I heard their concern. This demonstrates that I was listening to them. There went a click on the trust scale! I told them that my schedule tends to be full. Hey! This guy must be pretty damn good at what he does. He's in high demand! Now the person is thinking: "Dang, I want someone who is in demand." I shared that my clients are highly motivated individuals who desire to meet their goals, much like the ones they have. OOOOOOooooooo. See what I did there? I told them that I work with highly motivated people. Nobody wants to be made to feel like they aren't motivated, even if they are not. Notice I didn't tell them that they were not motivated. They just don't want me to think that they are not motivated. Finally, I said that my clients have dreams and aspirations just like them. JUST. LIKE. THEM. Everybody wants to be picked for the kickball team, right? They want to gain success just like all of my other clients.

The reason that I offer the Discovery Visit when needed is that, again, some people just need a little bit more value before they are willing to buy. Balking at the price is a common objection from people – over anything.

Remember, when someone calls you, they are already telling you that they want to buy. It is your job to uncover enough value for them to pull the trigger. By offering the Discovery Visit, I create the opportunity for me to be in front of them. This is an opportunity in which I am able to execute my Gift. The potential client can see me in person. They can touch me. Smell me. I give myself the chance to provide an example of a higher level of service that, perhaps, is new to them. And, I get to do so in their home where it is all about them.

At the end of the Discovery Visit, I repeat what they have previously told me with regards to their struggles – their inner struggles – their goals and desires. Then I thank them for inviting me into their home for this opportunity - which is probably the second time I have thanked them, because I like to mention that in the beginning. And then I mention how pleasant it was for me to be able to be with them 1:1 during this hour and focus on them. Then... "Tell me again, about your therapy experience before." Or... "Is this similar to what you have experienced before?" Or... "Since you have never been to therapy, is this kind of what you expected with therapy based on what others have told you?"

Now the wheels are turning. I'm guessing that they have NOT experienced this before. Or, this was NOT what they were expecting, because they have heard about PT standing for "Pain and Torture." Perhaps they went to therapy and the therapist spent 10 minutes with them while supervising three to four other clients. They are not thinking: "Hmmm. He just spent all this time with me; in my own home. I was the star of the show. This makes me feel kind of special; almost like I'm a celebrity. I like this feeling. I want to feel like a celebrity!"

And you know what comes next?
They person says:
"You know, why don't we go ahead and plan for (X) number of sessions and see how it goes."

Happens pretty darn near every time.

Take Home Points

- Objections are usually the potential customer's way of saying: "I need for you to give me a little more first."
- A Discovery Visit allows you the opportunity to put yourself in front of the potential customer so that they can experience your uniqueness first hand.
- This is your one chance to make the person feel really special. And everyone likes to feel special.
- They have invited you into their home, so they are wanting to buy. Your job is to confirm for them that they DO want to buy from you.
- Refer to your other clients in a positive way that makes them say to themselves: "I want to be like them."

CONCLUSION:
PLAY BALL

The biggest hurdle I have to help people over is that of getting out of their own way. Virtually everyone has been engrained with the way of The Establishment, which, so often, shackles individuals from successfully getting ahead. At no point in the educational process are the subjects that I have written about discussed. Yet, these are important foundational topics that lay down the tracks for reaching YOUR pot of gold at the end of the rainbow.

It is my hope that I have been able to help those who may be struggling in whatever way with regards to finding the freedom that they desire. Success in anything starts with a dream. Dreams come from the mind. Dreams involve creativity. And creativity takes courage.

Now that the gray matter that is between the ears can function more clearly, it is time to start taking steps. Many books finish with "The End."
But, as Harry Carey would have famously said: "Play Ball!"

ABOUT THE AUTHOR

David Bayliff, PT, MPT is the owner of Bayliff Integrated Wellness, a mobile concierge practice serving Paradise Valley and North Scottsdale, AZ. He started his practice in 2013 after spending 19 years in a variety of out-patient orthopedic clinics. Burn out from the daily grind of long hours, high patient volume, and endless paperwork led David to his new journey. In 2018 David formed The Mobile PT League, a private Facebook group for healthcare providers. Since then, he has been a mentor and coach to many therapists from around the country. David's mission in his mobile concierge practice is to "bring the playground back into people's lives." He carries that same mission into his coaching business as he aims to help budding entrepreneurs to become the practitioners they envisioned when they made the decision to pursue their chosen career path. His thoughts written in The Winning Mindset for the Mobile Entrepreneur apply to anyone looking to build their own dreams – whether mobile or brick-and-mortar.

This book was written with the assistance of Jeremy Sutton of Healthy Books, LLC.

Jeremy is a physical therapist. He is the creator of Healthcare Self-Publishing Academy where he teaches healthcare providers how to become the seen authority in their profession and their region. Join the free Facebook group Healthcare Self-Publishing Academy to learn how to get your book written and published. To set up a discovery call on his website to learn how you can get your book done in 90 days.

Telling Your Story Starts Here

HEALTHCARE SELF PUBLISHING ACADEMY

WWW.HEALTHYBOOKS.NET

WWW.FACEBOOK.COM/SELFPUBLISHINGACADEMY

Made in the USA
San Bernardino, CA
17 January 2020